9

First Affections

WEST SUSSEX COUNTY LIBRARY

WITHDRAWN

He who has once been happy is for aye
Out of destruction's reach . . .
Time is his conquest. Life, if it should fret
Has paid him tribute . . .
He who has once been happy! . . .

In memory of my parents,
M. M. and F. H. G. ('Gardener G')

The author – aged 5

First Affections

Some autobiographical chapters
of early childhood

Eve Garnett

FREDERICK MULLER LTD
LONDON

Acknowledgements

The Frontispiece photograph of the author, aged five, was taken by her father – at 8 o'clock on a June morning. Also by him is the drawing reproduced on the Dedication page, originally one of several 'Decorations' to a Victorian-Edwardian photograph book.

Both photographs have been printed by Edward Reeves of Lewes, Sussex.

WEST SUSSEX LIBRARIES

Copy No.	Class No.	B
4463384		GAR
Supplier	Date Invoiced	
WOOLSTONS	10 MAY 1985	
1st Loc.	Initials	2nd Loc.	Initials
XR	GAB	HN 11/87	CL
3rd Loc.	Initials	4th Loc.	Initials

WITHDRAWN

First published in Great Britain 1982 by
Frederick Muller Limited, Dataday House,
8 Alexandra Road, London SW19 7JU

Copyright © 1982 Eve Garnett

All rights reserved. No part of this publication may be reproduced, stored in a retrieval system, or transmitted, in any form or by any means, electronic, mechanical, photocopying, recording or otherwise, without the prior permission of Frederick Muller Limited.

British Library Cataloguing in Publication Data

Garnett, Eve
  First affections.
  1. Devon (England)—Social life and customs
  2. Worcestershire (England)—Social life and customs.
  I. Title
  942.3'5082'0924   DA670.D5

  ISBN 0-584-11003-0

Photoset by Rowland Phototypesetting Limited
Bury St Edmunds, Suffolk
Printed and bound in Great Britain at
The Camelot Press Ltd, Southampton

Contents

By the same author

For children
THE FAMILY FROM ONE END STREET
FURTHER ADVENTURES OF THE FAMILY FROM ONE
    END STREET
HOLIDAY AT THE DEW DROP INN – A ONE END
    STREET STORY
A BOOK OF THE SEASONS: AN ANTHOLOGY
TO GREENLAND'S ICY MOUNTAINS – THE STORY OF
    HANS EGEDE, EXPLORER, COLONISER,
    MISSIONARY, with a Foreword by Professor N. Egede
    Bloch-Hoell, University of Oslo
Illustrations to the Puffin edition of Stevenson's
A CHILD'S GARDEN OF VERSES
IN AND OUT AND ROUNDABOUT – STORIES OF A
    LITTLE TOWN
LOST AND FOUND – Four stories

For adults
IS IT WELL WITH THE CHILD? with a Foreword by Walter
    de la Mare

Preface

SOME OF THESE chapters of autobiography were originally written for a friend whose children 'wished to
know about the author as a little girl'. They have been added
to over the years and have been read by others, known and
unknown, nearly all of whom have expressed a wish for their
publication. A well-known writer once said that to imagine
one's infant doings could be of interest outside one's immediate circle demanded a certain modicum of conceit. It has also
been frequently asserted that the early years of any autobiography are the most interesting. While largely in agree-
ment with both these statements, today I think there is a
third matter for consideration. The war of 1914 changed for
ever the whole pattern of living in England. A way of life was
swept away – never to return. Those who were children
immediately before or during that period will soon have left
us. What they saw, felt, or did, however trivial or uneventful,
will then belong to history. And so it is as history I offer these
small rememberings, these 'First Affections' to a wider
public.

Eve Garnett

CHAPTER 1

'From quiet home and first beginning . . .'

MY CHILDHOOD WAS spent between Worcestershire where I was born, and Devon where we went for most of our holidays, and, for a time, to live.

My birthplace was a small hamlet just above the River Teme, not far from its junction with the Severn. It was very much the 'pastoral heart of England'; a rich, fertile, but flat and rather shapeless countryside. Farms; field after field – often with great groups of elms and of park-like dimensions – given over to grazing; acres of hop-yards; acres of orchards – plum, cherry, and apple; the only break in the flatness the humped outline of the Malvern Hills, glimpsed far away on the horizon between trees and tall hedges.

My two sisters were separated in age by just over thirteen months; between myself and the younger was a gap of nearly nine years. When I was two-and-a-half we moved to a house on the outskirts of the nearby Cathedral town for what my mother always referred to as 'this dreadful education business'. She had strong prejudices and education, anyway beyond the three Rs, was one of them. How much this was due to her own experience I do not know. She used to speak with a mixture of awe and horror about the boarding school at Clifton to which her father, suddenly aware that after four years an English governess had failed to eradicate their rich Irish brogue, dispatched his three daughters.

For economy they travelled by cattle boat, crossing three times a year from Waterford to Bristol. I used to love to hear about these voyages which, chaperoned only by the cattle, were made in the exuberant company of young gentlemen from Clifton College and were apparently the sole happiness in three years of purgatory. A purgatory only equalled by six months at an establishment near Paris where the inadequacy of the food matched that of the drains and from which my mother returned to Ireland, her face covered in sores resolutely determined never to go back. And go back she did not. Her sisters, of tougher physical but weaker moral fibre, meekly returned to endure – and survive – another six months but she stood her ground, defied Papa, and flatly refused to accompany them.

Defying Papa took courage. Though fond of him – and he of her – I have reason to suspect she was his favourite daughter – and he doubtless considered himself a devoted, even an indulgent parent, and in many ways was a just and kind one – he was an autocrat of autocrats, the epitome of Victorian parenthood. For weeks after this declaration of independence, both in Ireland and in London, where the family now spent part of the year, life was made intolerable for everyone. But Papa had met his match. Gradually the affair blew over. Seven years later my mother was to defy him again for after enduring nearly four years of a forbidden but firmly held-to engagement to my father, they were married one foggy November morning by Special Licence. The ceremony took place at the barbarous hour of eight a.m., my father kneeling at the altar displaying ten-and-sixpence in white chalk on the soles of his hastily purchased shoes; the only member of my mother's family present, her youngest sister – shaking with terror, and chaperoned by the housekeeper.

When I was seven, my sisters now at a boarding school, we went to live in Devon, returning at the end of five years to the same hamlet – though not the same house – where I was born. Here I finished my growing-up.

The later memories in the chapters that follow are concerned mainly with the years in Devon; the earlier with the house 'on the outskirts of the nearby Cathedral town', an old Georgian house with a vast surrounding garden.

And what an enchanting garden it was! To me, recently introduced to Eden, it was Eden indeed! I knew exactly where the Lord God walked at Even – in the Long Grass – a kind of wild jungle beyond the tennis courts, or sometimes, on still summer evenings or Saturday afternoons when the gardener had gone home, beside the Ranunculus bed at the top of the kitchen garden . . . As for the Tree of the Knowledge of Good and Evil, it stood, a glowing Arbutus outside the dining room windows, and the fruit thereof was strictly forbidden – to children and grown-ups alike – so that there was no possible doubt as to its identity. I knew too, and could have shown anyone the exact spot (though I never did, being shy in these matters) where Christ appeared to St Mary Magdalen: it was just beside the little round rockery by the bee-hives – though how she could have mistaken Him for the gardener I was never able to understand – gardeners in my experience, being clothed always in dark blue serge trousers, shiny as to the knees and behind, striped shirts, heavy boots, and cloth caps – a costume completely at variance with the flowing robes and sandals so faithfully depicted in 'The Good Shepherd' and other biblical nursery literature.

But while I was familiar with the Gospel stories, I was fairly steeped in the Old Testament. The goings out and the comings in of the chief characters of the Pentateuch and the Books of Samuel and Kings, occupied all my walks abroad. The sites of innumerable Israelite camps, the hill where Lot's lingering wife looked back and met her tragic doom, the very pit into which the jealous sons of Jacob thrust their boasting brother – all were identified. Esau and Jacob, David and Goliath, Balaam and his Ass mingled happily with characters from Hans Andersen, Grimm and the tales of Beatrix Potter. Noah and his Ark, Great Claus and his four horses, Mr MacGregor and his garden – all were contemporary. Stranger things happened in God's garden than Mr MacGregor's it seemed, but for villainy, between Cain or Joseph's brethren and some of the less pleasing characters in the fairy tales there appeared little to choose. Nor was there anything even remotely surprising in the conversations of the Serpent or even the vocal prowess of Balaam's Ass to one to whom the chatterings of Peter Rabbit and his cousin Benjamin, or the homilies of Mrs Tiggy-Winkle were as normal and familiar as the blue-rimmed nursery tea cups.

* * * * *

The old house is gone now. Six perky bungalows stand on the site. The Walnuts, the Copper Beech, the Arbutus – all are gone. The kitchen garden is part of an allotment; 'intensive' hens scratch in the Ranunculus bed; and in the Long Grass (where the Lord God walked at Even) stands a red sandstone church. . . . Does he walk there I wonder?

CHAPTER 2

'Their scent survives their close . . .'

1 Honeysuckle

'TIS WONDERFUL,' said the old lady sniffing a bunch of mixed flowers as she waited on a bench at a dusty surburban station, 'how the scents do take one back'. Her companion looked at her vaguely. The evocative power of scent evidently meant nothing to her. The old lady turned to me and smiled and I smiled back, confident in the free-masonry of those who carry their childhood always with them, and whose first encounters are etched deep into their being. For to most of us how potently evocative is the power of scent! How miraculously, in a split second, one can be wafted back in time, into a less crowded and clamorous world; a world where skies are quiet and even the winter mud and summer dust are somehow cleaner. Scents; smells, pleasant and unpleasant; one could name a hundred! To me perhaps flower scents are among the most potent, punctuating as it were, all the early years of child-hood.

Honeysuckle is, I think, my earliest flower memory. I am three-years-old and being lifted up to smell it growing up the wall and under the thatch of a white-washed cottage in Devon. How we had reached this outpost – for the cottage stood quite alone in a narrow, high-hedged lane with apparently no other habitation for miles, is a blank. But I remember the scorching heat, the sun burning through my cotton dress – even through the crown of my panama hat, and, very distinctly, the long grey shadows in the dusty little lane. The owner of the cottage, a very old lady in a black dress, white apron, and faded mauve print sun-bonnet looks on with pride. Larger and more luxuriant sprays are pointed out and directed to be pulled forward for me to smell. The scent is so strong I am almost anaesthetised. The old lady nods in pleasure but warns of the presence of bees. I am lifted down – half doped but protesting – and admonished by my attendant, the then reigning nursery governess, to say 'thank you' to the old lady. After staring dumbly, kindly attributed to shyness, and further prompting, the thanks are duly spoken. I beg to be lifted up again but this is denied; 'it is getting on for bedtime'. These ominous and all too familiar words end this brief encounter. But I never smell Honeysuckle without being instantly aware of that thatched cottage; the old lady in her black dress, white apron, and faded mauve sun-bonnet; the long shadows in the dusty little lane, and the sun scorching through my dress and the top of my panama hat.

2 Bluebells

My next flower memory is the following year. It is spring and, again late afternoon. We were now living on the outskirts of the Cathedral town already mentioned. Quite a short walk brought one to rural surroundings; fields, farms, and the black and white cottages of that countryside. There was also, at what appeared to me an immense distance away, a small wood to which – or so it seemed – we were always going but never went.

Now, at last, with my two sisters and a well-loved and remembered nursery governess, we were on our way – 'to see the Bluebells'. The prospect of the wood excited me – but not the Bluebells. I had already seen them; limp, drooping, sheaves – more like animal fodder than flowers, with long white, unnatural looking stems, carried in the arms of the townspeople who passed under our high garden wall on early-closing day, or even more forlorn, wilting on the bicycle carriers of Sunday excursionists, and I had not been impressed.

I remember nothing of what must have been quite a long walk to the wood, only of approaching it and being lifted over a high stile. I remember that beyond the stile stretched trees – seemingly to infinity, and that under them, amazingly, the

6

ground was blue! And yet not blue. . . I could not name the colour. Even today no word seems to me adequate to describe it. I stood gazing, gazing. Only when I heard my sisters exclaiming did I realise the 'blue' was flowers – bluebells!

A narrow path ran between the trees and they were even growing there; you could not walk without treading on them – and one did not tread on flowers. . . The younger of my sisters picked a few, sniffed them, apparently with deep satisfaction, then held them out to me. 'Smell!' she commanded briefly. I obeyed. Both their scent and their little hanging bells enchanted me. I began picking the flowers myself – feverishly, greedily. . . . The rest of the party moved slowly on, picking a flower here and there as they went and finally disappearing round a bend in the path. I continued picking and sniffing alternately. Suddenly the sun which had been intermittent burst out, shining brilliantly. Its warmth sent wave after wave of the Bluebell smell as I called it, wafting towards me. From that moment I was lost, intoxicated. I made a sudden rush to where the flowers grew thickest, and like a young animal rolled and rolled in ecstasy among them, ravished alike by their scent and by their beauty.

The incident was not popular. I remember being called – several times – and not answering; someone coming to look for me; the words 'naughty', and 'the ground is damp'; and being told, 'Look what you have done to the poor Bluebells!' And I remember standing and staring at the crushed and flattened flowers. But without remorse; possessor and possessed.

*   *   *   *   *

Over half a century has gone by, but every spring, when I catch the scent from a drift of Bluebells for the first time, for a brief second I am my four-year-old self again, rolling in ecstasy among them.

Large clumps of Primroses grew beside the four big aspar-
agus beds made by a previous tenant in our kitchen garden.
There were also some deep reddish-pink Polyanthus. Here
and there, presumably a mixture of the two, grew other
Primroses – definitely Primroses for they were always single-
stemmed – of a pale, pinkish brown. 'The Bloody Primroses'
I had christened them. I liked matching things and the
flowers seemed to me the exact colour of the dried, faded
blood on the handkerchiefs so often to be seen encircling my
knees after some cut or graze had been duly washed and
dealt with.

'The Bloody Primroses are out!' I remember announcing
and rushing excitedly towards my father holding out a newly
picked bunch of them. I can still see his look of rather
horrified astonishment, hear his sharp, 'Hush! Hush! You
mustn't say that word.' My own voice falteringly demanding, 'Why? Why *not*?' And his, 'Because it's not a nice word
and you mustn't say it. Promise!'

He so seldom spoke sharply that I realised it was something that mattered – and mattered a lot; like his firm
insistence on always speaking the truth, or, in nursery
language, of never, *never* telling a story. He explained no
further. I promised and the word was immediately associated in my mind with 'messy' – as my cut knees were
frequently described. At that period, it was not, as today, a
word used by all and sundry, especially in the presence of
women – much less children. It was many years before I
learnt its real meaning. . . .

But 'garden' Primroses were one thing; wild ones – 'whole
woods and fields full' I was promised, – were another, and
one perfect April morning a strange procession came out of
our front gate heading for the country. Leading the procession was my father; attached to his bicycle a kind of wicker-
work Bath chair, hired for the occasion, in which I sat
enthroned, a cushion at my back, a rug over my bare knees, a
large empty basket on my lap and a picnic basket at my feet.
Immediately behind was my mother. Her bicycle boasted a
carrier and to this was strapped another large and empty

basket. Behind her, side by side, came my sisters each with an empty bicycle basket attached to their handlebars. Last of all came 'the Grunter' – Miss Grundy, whose brief stay with us is described in Chapter 5. She, too, had a carrier with a large basket but not entirely empty, for it held a pair of scissors and a ball of wool. For what might be called this primrose raid was not for ourselves but destined for a London hospital, and we had had a very early lunch in order to return in time to pack and post them. Posts then were sure – and speedy. By about nine o'clock next morning our Primroses would, as Tennyson wrote in perhaps one of his less-inspired moments, '. . . Freshen and sweeten the wards, like the waft of an angel's wing.'

Our destination was six miles away but in a little over a mile we were already in rural surroundings. The hedges, and the huge elms characteristic of that part of the county were in their full but still light-green leafage. Here and there big patches of Primroses could be seen and I waved excitedly at them as we went by. But when we finally reached our destination and, a five-barred gate opened, bumped over ruts and grass to disembark on what might be described as the promised land, for a moment or two I could not believe what I saw was really true! The grass of the high-sloping bank that formed one side of the field and the ground of the little copse immediately above it were almost, in places entirely, hidden by Primroses; a pale, luminous, creamy-yellow carpet. . .

Lifted out of my curious conveyance, clutching my empty basket I was about to rush headlong towards them but was stopped by a restraining hand, commanded to stand still – and *listen*; then solemnly abjured to pick long-stemmed primroses *only*! A very necessary warning for I was given, out of enthusiasm for some newly-opened or desirable bloom, to doing very much the reverse.

An hour – perhaps an hour and a half of steady picking; a picnic tea, then home; the sun, lower in the sky but still warmly shining and every basket filled with bunches of Primroses, each with a few leaves and tied round with wool, ready to be packed.

Even from a single Primrose there is a faint but ambrosial scent. In a bunch it is ineffable – unforgettable. And unforgotten; for every spring since that long ago April day I have only to smell the first Primrose of the year and I am instantly transported to a sloping sunny bank, sniffing at a bunch of Primroses destined for a London'hospital.

4 *Convolvulus*

There are many people I believe who dislike – even loathe – the smell of Convolvulus; better known to some as Bindweed, or, to the more scientifically minded, as *Convolvulus Arvensis*. To me it is not only the sweetest of scents but one of the most potently evocative. I am five-years-old and we are spending my sisters' school holidays at a tiny village on the north coast of Brittany. The so-called 'Hôtel' – five shillings-a-day inclusive, with its excellent food, swarms of flies, and far from pleasantly evocative smells – typhoid broke out later and we left hurriedly – was some distance from the sea. To a five-year-old whose sole idea was to reach the small sandy beach, or was returning tired out after a morning of ceaseless activity spent on it, it seemed a long hot trek. And it *was* hot; August sun in Brittany can be very powerful indeed.

The way lay along a rough track over sandy ground; not actual sandhills until one approached the beach itself but more sand than soil. The ground was so hot that it almost scorched bare feet and penetrated uncomfortably and impartially through British sand-shoes or French espadrilles. But there was consolation; a consolation that never failed. Everywhere in the sandy soil and especially bordering the track, were great patches and trails of pink and white Convolvulus. The air was drenched with the honey-sweetness of their scent and to my amazed eyes over every patch and trail fluttered dozens of small blue butterflies while overhead hovered, literally, clouds of them! I had seen blue butterflies in my father's boy-hood collection at home but do not remember their making much impression on me. These were something quite different; something magical!

As we went along I could only bear to take my fascinated gaze from them to see if we were nearing the Mecca of the beach. . .

But the honey-sweet smell evokes other memories. Sometimes along the sandy track old women in black dresses and stiffly starched white Breton caps led cows to some, to me, unknown pasture. One day I was offered a ride as far as the beach. My mother at first demurred but finally yielded to my entreaties. I was lifted up and remember vividly the unexpected *width* of the cow – and the intense discomfort of its backbone sticking into me. But the thrill, the pride! '*I* rode on a cow in France,' I boasted to young friends on our return home. All looked suitably impressed. Except Hubert. Hubert was a 'special' friend. A noisy and exuberant child, a few years older than myself. I valued his esteem; to me he seemed a fount of knowledge and experience. He had a bicycle, a garden of his own, a German governess; he even spoke German. Alas, he was not only unimpressed – he refused to believe me. Fortunately I had my mother as witness. Convinced, Hubert magnanimously expressed admiration – even envy. Honour was satisfied.

The Convolvulus scent lasted all the way to the sandhills; sometimes you could even smell it on the beach and see little companies of blue butterflies fluttering by. The beach itself, a small crescent-shaped bay of fine, smooth sand, sloped steeply. This was a disadvantage for all of us for it made bathing dangerous for non-swimmers, and for small children – out of their depth in a few steps – impossible. My sisters – then nearly fourteen and fifteen, could swim a little, but it was decreed no one might bathe unless my father was present. Though a very strong swimmer – many years before he had rescued a young man being swept towards the dreaded Morte current off the north Devon coast and had subsequently been awarded the Royal Humane Medal – the experience had left him nervous and apprehensive for others. My sisters practised their swimming under his eye – and well within their depth, but for me only paddling in a few inches of water was permitted. But such was my anguish at this deprivation – for to bathe was the high-light – almost a celestial high-light one might say – of a holiday at the sea – that he substituted what I now think a strangely dangerous alternative. For once without protest I allowed myself to be buttoned into a 'passed on' – and long out-dated – bathing dress, once the property of my second sister.

The tyranny of 'passed on' clothes; their apparently inexhaustible capacity for wear! A tyranny, to one who grew slowly, made no more bearable by the knowledge that when the offending garment finally wore out – or became too small – there waiting, was its fellow, a size larger, belonging to the other sister.

Clad in this garment I would sit astride my father tightly clutching the neck of his dark blue bathing dress or holding on to what I described as his 'fat' – he was a well-covered man – while he swam out from shore. Admittedly no great distance – perhaps fifty or sixty yards – but in very deep water, back and forth the length of the little bay we would go. Blue sky, blue sea; little waves washing over one's legs; sea-gulls sweeping by; to me it was complete rapture, unutterable bliss; and I think my father enjoyed it too. Yet how easily some accident might have occurred! Cramp for instance? No one else could swim adequately; there were rarely other people on the beach; there was no boat . . .

When the tide ebbed a line of seaweed and shells remained. Beautiful shells – especially the kind we called 'fans'. These ranged in colour from a deep rust red to palest pink; almost always unblemished and sometimes 'double' – as they seldom were in England. And then one day 'The Shell' as it came to be called, was found.

'S'wark', pronounced 'S'work' – a corruption of her surname – our last and most dearly loved governess – was the finder. The shell lay all by itself at the very end of the sandy crescent. It was so beautiful that she called my sisters and myself to see it before she actually picked it up. It was not large; perhaps a little over an inch in width and slightly more in length. It was a 'double' shell with a delicately grooved surface, and a crinkly edge without chip or blemish – perfect. But it was its colour – even dried by the sun – for the colour of all shells is more intense when wet – that, anyway for us, was unique. Except for a few dark purple spots it was a strange, deep, pinkish mauve; and it glowed as if polished. We took it home in triumph, showing it to everyone we met but nobody had seen one like it. Even the old Professor from the Sorbonne who lived near and sometimes arrived attired in a bathing-dress of Victorian design and an enormous straw hat turned up at the side, to invite my father and sisters to go prawning, was impressed. Could it, I now wonder, have been a tropical shell; an alien that had drifted northwards from some far off and warmer sea?

Blue butterflies; astride my father's back in a blue sea; riding on a cow; an alien shell; the memory of 'passed on' clothes; an old Professor in a huge straw hat. . . . Memories, unchanged and changeless, all instantly evoked by one sniff of a small, wild Convolvulus flower.

5 Lilies of the Valley

These were considered very special – almost exotic – flowers; somewhere in the same class as Mimosa, Malmaison carnations or Gloire-de-Dijon roses. Why this should have been so I have no idea. They grow wild in many parts of England; few old gardens are without them; they are hardy and, once established, multiply rapidly. They grew prolifically in our garden but were very definitely reserved for grown-ups and children were forbidden to pick them. To me they were essentially 'party' flowers. Grown-ups wore large bunches of them on festive occasions pinned to the lapels of coats or the bosoms of dresses – especially evening dresses. Their powerfully evocative scent immediately recalls my mother in a black lace dress, wearing a bunch of them, bending over my bed to kiss me goodnight on her way downstairs to take a last look at the dining-room table before guests for a dinner party should arrive; and the memory of that same table, changed out of all recognition from its everyday appearance, shown me an hour or so earlier. Table napkins in fantastic shapes; the best dessert dishes filled with pears and grapes; the marvel of a pineapple; above all, little silver dishes full of 'petit fours' and unknown but delectable looking sweets, one or two of which I know will be 'saved' for me and found on the chair by my bed next morning . . .

Equally, if not more vividly the scent evokes another kind of festivity – garden parties – and a small incident connected with one of these. This form of entertainment lingered on in rural areas up to the time of the Second World War, perhaps today's cocktail party is the nearest equivalent. A convenient and – relatively – inexpensive way of entertaining a large number of guests at one and the same time. 'Killing them off' was the surprising formula used – surprising to a child that is – until explained.

Unlike the cocktail party, garden parties required far more preparation beforehand. We were living at this time in the old Georgian house mentioned earlier. It was a particularly delightful house for children having the broad corridors and some rooms – the nursery and my sisters' bedroom among them – with the small 'powdering rooms' of the period leading off them. These little rooms provided additional, almost private, play space; little lairs where nursery surprises were born and schoolroom plots and enterprises hatched. There was also a large expanse of flat roof to which access was forbidden except under adult supervision but was frequently – though furtively – visited by my sisters and their school-friends. But it was the garden that mattered most. Laid out in the spacious days of the Georgian era many of the trees must have been planted long before the house itself was built – there was probably an earlier one on the same site. Four great Walnuts, some of the largest I have ever seen, stood together on the main lawn. A magnificent cedar shaded a small triangular patch of grass – my principal playing place. A tall and very lovely Copper Beech grew in a hedge screening part of the vegetable garden, and outside the dining room windows the luxuriant Arbutus already referred to. A semi-circular yew hedge separated the main garden from the gravelled sweep by the front door. It was fourteen feet high or more with a wide archway cut in the centre and must have been at least two hundred-years-old. Some big, bosky Evergreen Oaks overshadowed the short, steep drive and several more grew above the long, high wall that bordered the main road. The wall at which poor S'wark, as she was so often to tell us later, had looked with such aversion as she drove alone from the station in a stuffy one-horse cab smelling faintly of hay and ammonia, to her first encounter with us.

Some kind of Institution she had finally decided, peering apprehensively from the cab as it rumbled slowly past and was just congratulating herself that her work at least lay with private families, when the cab suddenly turned, slowed up, and came to a halt before a pair of forbidding-looking iron gates and to her dismay the driver climbed down to open them. But her dismay was short-lived for in less than a minute the steep drive turned a corner, the house came into view and they drew up at the front door. The steps under the high, white-pillared porch were gay with round green tubs of blue Agapanthus, and on either side was a superb bed of Violas. A man in his shirt-sleeves was what she described as 'on his hunkers' absorbed in snipping off the dead flowers. The gardener she supposed. . . . And the gardener it was, though not what might be described as the official one, for it was my father, 'Gardener G', as she was later so aptly and endearingly to christen him.

My parents had leased this palatial property for three reasons: its almost incredibly low rent – there was only a four-year lease to run for a church was to be built on part of the land and further building likely; the easy access to an excellent school, and the asset, unusual near the centre of a big town, of so large and beautiful a garden – 'a paradise for children' as visitors were given to remarking – as indeed it was. Rather less paradisial, however, was its upkeep. Where the original owner had probably employed an out-door staff of three or four and his successors never less than two men and a boy, my father laboured – slaved is perhaps not too strong a word, with one semi-trained gardener; an individual of decided views and rather uncertain temper. Cutting the grass in summer – motor mowers were still mostly confined to public parks and large estates – was almost one man's work. Like painting the Forth Bridge no sooner finished than it was time to start again. In addition to two tennis courts there were other small lawns; various little squares, oblongs and triangles, and at the side of the house, overlooked by most of the principal rooms, a maddening expanse of grass in which some misguided person had cut small round, crescent, and heart-shaped beds. Besides the intricate mowing required to navigate between these, they also had, like innumerable gravel paths, to be neatly trimmed – 'edged' as it was called, with long stiff shears, monotonous and very tiring work as anyone who has done it will confirm. In addition all these little beds – and large ones too – had to be kept filled: in winter, so far as I remember, with Wallflowers; in summer with 'bedding outs'. This bedding out took place in late spring and was a major operation. The results were delightful but the labour, I now realise, must have been immense – especially as my father, for reasons of economy, grew everything possible from seed. The late-Victorian vogue for scarlet Geraniums, yellow Calceolarias, and a peculiarly hideous dark blue Lobelia, all planted in lines of military precision had been rigidly adhered to by our immediate predecessor. Only a long triangular-shaped bed near the Walnut trees had escaped. It was filled with sturdy little Azaleas – a relic of earlier Victorian – possibly even Georgian times; beautiful both to look upon and to smell.

My father had been determined to eradicate the Victorian flora as soon as possible. Now, on either side of the front door where flaming 'Paul Crempel', canary-coloured Calceolarias, and the hideous dark blue Lobelia had reigned supreme, the cool-looking Violas already mentioned, flourished. Only the tubs of Agapanthus beloved of Victorians and Edwardians alike, so disdained and derided by their successors, now fashionable once more, were allowed to remain. Sweet William, Canterbury bells, big white Daisies, Stocks and Pansies filled all other beds, with borders of Ageratum or of 'Mrs Simpkin' in place of the blue Lobelia.

In the kitchen garden other Victorian – and even pre-Victorian flowers and shrubs were allowed to remain undisturbed. Beside hedges, untidily bordering strawberry beds and cabbages, in the shade of trees, all bloomed and flourished in their seasons. Laurustinus and Lilacs; a Japonica with little yellow ball-like flowers know to us always as 'Prunes-and-Prisms'; the Primroses and Polyanthus mentioned earlier; Forget-me-nots and Pansies; 'everlasting' Sweet Peas; tall Doronicums; enchanting Moss-roses; what I would persist in calling 'Solemn-and-Seal' and, of course, Lilies of the valley – and all, except the Lilies, might be picked.

They were my joy, my loves. Every fine spring or summer morning, as soon as the hands of the night-nursery clock pointed to 7.15, I would wriggle myself into my vest, socks, and knickers. I could not tell the time, but I knew by the look of the hands when the hour had arrived. Before that I was not allowed to get up and conversation was discouraged. But now S'wark could be approached and asked to fasten the back of my blue-and-white striped overall – an ex- and very out-dated dress of a sister, and my white through-at-the-toes strap shoes. Then I would rush wildly from the house to see what new buds had opened, what hitherto unknown was what the gardener called 'showing for bloom'. Twenty minutes or so later, after rapturous exploring and picking I would return with a bunch of something, the all-too-short stems clutched tightly in a hot and grubby fist; the first-fruits of the morning – an offering for S'wark.

On garden party days I would assume the role of guide. I knew the names of all the flowers – Solemn-and-Seal was the only lapse – and I wanted everyone to see, admire and love them as I did. At this period I much preferred men to women. Women were inclined to rush at one, bestow unwanted kisses, and to make comments on blue eyes and party clothes. Men neither rushed nor kissed, and comments on one's clothes and appearance were made, if at all, off-stage.

'Come and see the Ranunculus' – I was very proud both of the flowers and their long name – I would command Captain F. from the nearby Barracks, or Doctor V. from the County Mental Hospital, or some other temporarily unattached male refreshing himself with lemonade after exertions on the tennis court (tennis was provided for the more energetic guests). And politely, whoever was asked, would down the remainder of his drink, take my hand, and off we would go.

Garden parties were rare events: two or at the most three, in any one summer. Apart from the necessary mowing of all grass, the marking-out of tennis courts and the extra tidying up involved, a fine day was very important for a really successful party. Once, either for some more than usually festive occasion, or doubts about the weather, a marquee had been hired; there were also to be ices. The era of the ubiquitous American-styled 'ice cream' had not yet arrived. Ices were a rarity, encountered only at Christmas parties and the very occasional visit to a tea-shop. My mother's invariable reply, 'I'll bring you back an ice in a paper-bag' to a request for something edible from a party or visit from home was as nearly related to reality as the Lapland woman's note on a dried cod in Hans Andersen's 'Snow Queen'; indeed for many years the two were closely associated in my mind.

It was evidently to be an extra-special party and for some reason, long since forgotten if indeed I ever heard it, my presence was not desired. The news was not broken until after lunch when my mother called me into her bedroom. A very stormy scene indeed ensued. Not only was my dignity affronted – I had never missed a garden party yet, but to add insult to injury, I was to go, at once, and get ready for a walk, thus implying I was not even to be on the premises when the guests arrived. And, above all, I was going to miss the marquee in all its glory – *and* the ices!

I remember weeping and stamping with fury, and finally flinging myself on the bed in an abandonment of misery. In vain I was assured I could come, as my sisters, busy with prep and practising, always did, after the last guests had departed, for cakes and lemonade, and, today, ices. Everything would be there, everything just the same . . .

It was no good. I knew, unerringly, nothing would be in the least the same, and, 'cakes and ale' apart, what about the flowers? Who would escort Captain F. and the others to see them? . . . And I continued to weep.

Finally my mother lost patience. I was picked up and dumped firmly on my feet. She held up a warning finger – a gesture usually presaging some ominous threat . . . Silenced for the moment, before I could protest further she produced a brown paper parcel. If I promised to make no more fuss, and to go, at *once*, to get ready for my walk its contents were mine. After some slight hesitation and much sniffing, the promise was given; the parcel handed me. Parcels were always a joy and filled with excitement I unwrapt it. Inside was a toy dog – a grey felt poodle. It was about ten inches long by eight inches high. Its grey felt body was smooth and tautly stuffed; its long, flapping ears and neatly curled tail were of black astrakhan and black astrakhan covered the lower half of each sturdy felt leg. But all was as nothing compared with a small red tongue which protruded sideways from its mouth. At this I gazed incredulously, then touched it wonderingly with my fore-finger. It was made of scarlet flannel; smooth, soft – and utterly convincing. . . .

Garden party, disappointment, offended dignity, all were instantly forgotten; one single and overmastering desire possessed me; to get ready as quickly as possible for my walk and take Puggy as I was to call him (I had never seen a poodle) with me.

Bribery and corruption? Certainly bribery – a practice not normally countenanced in our family. You did as you were told, though by no means always or immediately, and frequently there were tears and temper. If the latter went on too long you were threatened with 'a good smack' – why 'good' I could never understand – or being made to stand in the corner, yelling loudly if the former was administered, weeping forlornly if the latter. Sixpence, it is true, was promised for good behaviour at the dentist's but this was more in the nature of a reward. Corruption? To my infant mind it was Justice. Because of disappointment about the party you, quite rightly you considered, wept and made a fuss. If, you were told, you stopped and 'behaved' you would be given a present. You did so – and received Puggy; Puggy with his flapping ears, curling tail, and soft little red flannel tongue . . .

Puggy was long loved and became the third, and most important, member of a family – known collectively as 'the Watchhouses'; and like a vanished house and garden;

vanished lives, and a vanished way of life, he is instantly recalled by one sniff of a bunch of lilies of the valley.

6 Burnet Roses – Part I

As potentially evocative to me as any flower already named, is the scent of the Burnet Rose. Like the Convolvulus 'it grows best', according to flower books, 'in sandy or heath-like soils, mostly near the sea.' Unlike the Convolvulus of which I was first made aware in France, it was in England, in the North Devon village of my earliest remembered flower scent – Honeysuckle, that I came to know the Burnet Rose. Its 'habitat' – to borrow again from a flower book, was in the short turf and on the lee side of the steeply sloping sand hills that divided the sea and the beach – two and a half miles of firm unblemished sand – from the garden of the one and only hotel – an expensive and exclusive establishment, and the small golf-course adjoining it. Though the golf-course was not a private one, it abounded in notices of the 'keep off' and 'beware of' variety and young children were not popular there. Noise – of any kind – especially shouting, was firmly discouraged. Occasionally someone would wander on to the fairway or stray too close to a green where some elderly gentleman was engaged in a life and death putt. There would be plenty of shouting then – but from adults . . .

At the time of which I write I do not remember this happening to myself; in later years – always in the forefront of any fracas and invariably the one to be "copped", yes; but now, at the age of seven, I was in charge of an adult and any wanderings in or near the area devoted mainly to searching for bee-orchis, occasionally found there. To me they were more strange than endearing flowers. It was the Burnet Rose that really mattered. The flowers, faintly creamy with a tinge of green in bud, a shining white with dazzlingly yellow stamens when fully out, had very thorny, prickly stalks which discouraged picking, and the flower itself wilted quickly in a hot hand. It was its ambrosial, intoxicating scent that drew and held one. The bushes were mostly short and stunted; you went down on your knees to them – in more senses than one perhaps, but the scent was all around. On a hot day with a slight breeze, waves of it would drift over the sand hills; over the golfers and flower seekers; sometimes as far as the village street . . . It was evocative even then, recalling the pleasures and enjoyments of both earlier and quite recent Devonian experiences – though it required little to evoke the six weeks of sheer bliss enjoyed by S'wark and myself the previous summer. Bliss for both, for S'wark, young, attractive, and delightful to look at, rather strangely introduced by me, had met and become engaged to her future husband.

We had come, she and I, for a kind of extended convalescence for me after measles earlier in the year. S'wark was an enthusiastic bather and we bathed every morning before breakfast, and often later in the morning as well. For the early bathe we would put macs over our bathing dresses, and clutching towels run down the short road from our lodgings, down some steep steps and along a path beside what was known as 'the Shelter,' a dispiriting kind of shed, open on three sides, roofed with corrugated iron and furnished with a long wooden bench where people huddled forlornly during sudden showers or thunder storms. Beyond it, more steep steps led down to a dry, dusty, and not very salubrious part of the beach where, later in the morning two rival 'Donkey Women' as they were called, would assemble with their respective steeds, and finally over cold, hard, but clean sand to what we called 'our rock'. This was a largish, flat-topped one standing alone and here unless the tide was very high we would leave our macs, shoes, and towels and make for the sea. Usually, at this hour, we had the beach almost to ourselves, but one morning, running back from a bathe a little ahead of S'wark, I was surprised to find two young men sitting on our rock. They had towels round their necks and were just about to take off their coats and shoes for a bathe. I was affronted; I had come to consider 'our rock' almost private property. I stood staring for a moment. The rock was not so very big and they were rather large young men.

'I'm hanged if there's any room for us here!' I announced loudly in an aggrieved voice to S'wark as she came up to me.

The young men stood up and began to make polite apologies. They were laughing and it later transpired they had mistaken my 'I'm hanged' for 'I'm damned' which, coming from a six-year-old in those days, amused them considerably. Actually the word was unknown to me though 'hanged' I had picked up from my father.

The two men were brothers; the elder a school-master, the younger just down from Oxford for the Long Vacation.

Actually the younger brother, who we were soon to know as Basil, had seen S'wark and myself before. He was staying with his parents, two grown-up sisters and one little nine-year-old one, in lodgings in the centre of the village. A few days drowsing on the beach had been enough to restore him after his labours at Oxford, and another four or five had been spent in exploring the immediate countryside. Apart from his family the only company available appeared to consist of elderly adults and small children and he was now frankly bored. Every afternoon he would walk up the steep two-and-a-half-mile long hill to the station, perching on a fence about half way up and hopefully scanning all newcomers arriving by the late afternoon train as they drove down to the village. It was while thus engaged, that he had noticed S'wark and myself. 'Mother and child' – our colouring was much the same – he had immediately assumed, 'and a very charming mother'!

A few days passed during which the elder brother had joined the family party. Both men were keen ornithologists; gulls, guillemots and other sea-birds were at the height of their nesting season and all day was spent climbing about the steep, jagged cliffs that jutted out to sea at what was known as The End of the Sands – an area always associated in my mind, and seemingly as inaccessible to me, as the end of the earth. But later in the morning of our bathing encounter Basil was on the beach with his family. We saw him talking earnestly to his mother and presently his nine-year-old sister coming towards us.

'My mother says,' she shyly asked S'wark, 'would your little girl like to build a house with me?'

While I stood staring and pondering the unfamiliar

'house', for with us all sand buildings were 'castles', S'wark had accepted for me. The nine-year-old then took my hand, and led us both to her family. Father, mother, and sisters were duly introduced, and our relationship duly explained by S'wark.

I do not remember the exact sequence of events that led up to the engagement but it must have been relatively soon, for long before the end of our four weeks allotted stay S'wark had written home to say I was benefitting so much from the good sea-air and would my mother consider our staying another two weeks, to which apparently she had readily agreed.

Chaperoned by me, Basil, and sometimes his brother, joined us for our early morning bathe, Basil always giving me what I called 'piggy-backs' up the steep flights of steps leading to our lodgings, and dumping me, not actually dripping but distinctly damp, at the gate. Ben, the elder brother, was engaged on some educational work in London before taking up a new appointment at a preparatory school in September, and only came down for a few days now and then. He too liked and admired S'wark and in later years was given to remarking that 'had he been permanently on the spot, Basil would not have had a look in!'

S'wark was an immediate favourite with the rest of the family. There were daily meetings on the beach; bathing, shrimping, shell-hunting expeditions, the building of sand-castles – I remained adamant about 'castles' – of all shapes and sizes. One enormous structure I remember particularly. It was built by Ben, Basil and their father to await a very high tide. It was five or six feet high and half a dozen or more of us were able to crowd on to it. There was also the near-miracle of finding its remains still there next morning; a huge circular mound, smooth and flattened and its, to me, exact resemblance to a gigantic saucer-pudding – a frequent, and favourite – feature of our landlady's excellent cooking!

There were many picnics. One to which I had greatly looked forward was to the End of the Sands. The younger members of the party, in charge of Basil's mother, travelled in Mrs Watson's donkey cart which, together with Mrs Watson and an enormous iron kettle could be hired for the afternoon. Mrs Watson, wearing a black dress, white apron, and a black straw hat adorned with many black ribbon bows, drove the donkey, and the rest of the party cheerfully tramped the two-and-a-half miles of hard, not-so-hard, and very heavy-going soft sand.

Our destination, when we finally reached it, seemed indeed the End of the Earth. No human beings were visible, and the only sounds the lapping or sudden splash of waves, the cries of sea-birds, and, from very far away, the occasional bleating of sheep. Alas, it was soon made abundantly plain that, for children, no venturing on to even the smooth boulders at the foot of the jagged cliffs which now seen close at hand loomed terrifyingly high, and apparently stretched seawards to infinity, was to be permitted. The nesting birds, the mysterious caves – even the sight of a seal – of which we had been told so much, were to remain as before; remote and inaccessible; yet another realm reserved exclusively for grown-ups!

The gathering of wood and the boiling of the huge iron kettle for tea, helped to make up for some of the disappointment but I remember a feeling of having been somehow defrauded; the End of the Sands was definitely out of favour . . .

Equally memorable – but utterly satisfying – was a whole day's picnic – a lunch and tea affair – at a sandy-bayed estuary twelve miles or so away. For this we drove in a waggonette – my first – and last – experience of one, Ben and Basil going on ahead of us on bicycles. The waggonette belonged to one, Mr Tarr, who sat proudly aloft, arrayed in a short cream-coloured coat and black straw boater, behind a pair of dark brown and very glossy-coated horses. His passengers were accommodated facing each other on two narrow bench-like seats cushioned in navy blue cloth punctuated with big cloth buttons to match. Mr Tarr kept strictly to the main road until nearing our destination it forked and we drove for a time beside flat, marsh-like land intersected with narrow dykes full of beautiful yellow Iris. It was the first time I had seen any and I was as enchanted with them as with the strange fact that they actually *grew* in water!

'Ah! Flaggers!' my mother had said, using the Irish name, when I spoke of them on our return home, and henceforth for me Flaggers they became – and have remained ever since.

The weather – perfect for most of our stay – on this particular day suddenly became quite cold; a chilly wind sprang up followed by a sharp shower just after we arrived and we ate our picnic lunch huddled against some sheltering cliffs. Later the sun came out but after tea the sky showed signs of darkening again and an early start for home was decided upon. Reluctantly Mr Tarr consented to take a shorter route and we drove up, down, and along narrow twisting lanes. I was disappointed at not seeing the Iris again, but was to be more than compensated.

The North Devon Foxglove season was at its height. The Foxgloves grew sparsely in our countryside. I rarely saw them but they held a strange fascination for me. They seemed to have – and indeed still do – an air of mystery about them; a cold aloofness; responsive only to clamorous bees. And now, suddenly, we were in a land of Foxgloves! In the high Devon hedges, singly or in groups, they dominated all other flowers, or could be glimpsed, standing like silent sentinels in the occasional pine woods. There were small, slender ones with pale half-opened buds; bright pink ones in full and lusty bloom; giants three to four feet high, more than half their lower petals already shed . . .

At first I was – literally – struck dumb. But not for long! Soon my ecstatic cries of '*Look!* Look at *that* one! Look at *those!*' were being echoed by the rest of the party. Ben and Basil were kept busy hopping off their bikes and armed with stout horn-handled pen-knives, vying with each other to cut the best specimens; S'wark and I were soon half-smothered in Foxgloves.

*　*　*　*　*

I do not remember the engagement being made known – only that it had 'happened' – it was not announced at home until our return there. I remember that we spent more time with Basil and his family and that the weather remained idyllic; all was as before. Only in the long, light evenings was there a difference. Then, safely in bed and asleep; the nightly ritual of an inch-square segment of rather gritty chocolate – the only kind available in the village – left beside my bed; the austere but kindly landlady installed on guard, S'wark and Basil were able to meet; to wander alone together in fields and lanes for an hour or so in the long-lingering July twilight . . . And waking early in the morning, sometimes, beside the gritty chocolate, would be a strange shell, or a sea-bird's feather; and once, a little vase filled with Water Forget-me-nots – Tennyson's

> . . . sweet Forget-me-nots
> That grow for happy lovers . . .

Burnet Roses – Part 2

And now a little less than a year – a year of constant changes – happy and unhappy – we were back. The changeless burnet rose was just coming into flower and intermittently one caught a breath of its unforgettable, intoxicating scent.

S'wark and I had hardly arrived home the previous July before the wind of change began to blow. Even I had known that 'one day' a church was to be built in 'the Long Grass' – a small jungle in our garden already referred to. Apparently this building might soon begin; any renewal of our four-year lease, due to terminate that autumn, could only be for a very limited period and as my sisters were going to a boarding school in September my parents had decided a move must be made. There was also an urgent need for economy. 'This dreadful education business' was continually on my mother's lips. The expense! . . . The fees! . . . the uniform! . . . the *extras*! . . . The last named calling forth particularly vehement denunciation.

I had known before S'wark and I went to Devon that my sisters were going 'away' to a new school – a boarding school – in September. It was clear going away meant being away day and night, but a boarding school? I could only visualise it as one huge, long, narrow room where people slept in rows on completely bare boards – similar to those in my play-room – but sloping slightly upwards, the spaces between each board as clearly defined as lines in an exercise book. But in June, at six-years-old, September is a long, long way off. It was only when I actually saw my sisters trying on the new school uniform – garments of a peculiarly hideous green – that I fully realised their departure was really near.

In spite of many differences of opinion; of teasing; of accusations of being spoilt, and the constantly reiterated '*we* were never allowed to do that!' In spite of taunts of 'consecrated dish' when something had to be specially cooked because a particular meal was unsuited to my years; or the hoots of mirth that always greeted what my mother invariably referred to as 'the child's last meal' – meaning my bedtime biscuits and milk – I was devoted to my sisters, and indeed they to me. The thought of not seeing them every day and all day Saturdays and Sundays was not to be endured. Something had to be done – and quickly. I thought hard. A year or so later a prayer at bedtime might have been considered but at this age prayers were more or less a routine, formal and said aloud. There was no private communing with Heaven . . . Then a fairy-story someone had once read to me came into my mind. It was about a water-sprite and though I was uncertain what a water-sprite was, I remembered she lived in a stream and that people went there with requests for help. Some even wrote their petitions, casting them into the water and waiting hopefully for her to surface.

I lost no time. Unlike reading and spelling, writing had never been any difficulty while actual letter-writing, thanks to Christmas and birthday 'thank you' missives, held no terrors for me though my spelling was, and still is, of the variety sometimes politely described as 'phonetic'. I remember the words of my letter though not the spelling.

'Dear Miss Stream,' I wrote, 'Please don't let R. and B.' – using their pet names – 'go away to school.'

Fortunately I knew of a stream within easy walking distance. In an almost rural setting it flowed beside a path through some fields – a short cut to the local barracks. It was a favourite walk and there was no opposition about us going there. About half-way, where the stream, never very deep, was wide and shallow, I lagged behind, and unseen, success-

27

fully dropped the letter, now folded in half and addressed 'Miss Stream', into the water. On our return I peered anxiously ahead and at first thought my request had been received. But alas, as we came nearer I could see it was still there, caught in some reeds near the bank. I lagged behind again and retrieved it and was about to throw it further out when S'wark turned and called to me to 'come away from the stream and come along'. As I did not obey she called again and finally the younger of my sisters came running to fetch me.

'What are you doing there – getting all muddy – and what's that in your hand?' she demanded. 'You shouldn't pick up dirty bits of paper,' and she added a popular formula of the day, 'you don't know where it's been!'

'I *do*!' I said angrily triumphant as she grabbed it from me and I tried to grab it back. But she held it out of my reach and seeing writing proceeded to read it. Her face softened and I think she was touched, but 'you little silly!' was all she said – and pocketed the letter. I remember dissolving into tears but was not unduly upset. Belief in Miss Stream and her powers had not been completely whole-hearted . . .

I made up for it a few days later, wailing loudly and considerably embarrassing my whole family at the station when we went to say goodbye.

*　　*　　*　　*　　*

Little time was left for repining. The very day after my sisters had departed 'packing up' began in earnest. During the next ten days or so chaos reigned. Chairs denuded of their chintzes stood looking naked and forlorn. Beds not in use were heaped high with blankets, and with pillows and bolsters in unfamiliar striped covers. Pictures leant against walls instead of hanging on them; china and glass stood on the floor or herded together on tables, and in most of the rooms windows were curtainless, carpets and rugs rolled up.

In the midst of all the upheaval the house agent was constantly bringing prospective short-term tenants to see over the property. On one occasion I had been 'put in the corner' by S'wark for some misdemeanour. Probably owing to the general disorder, the only corner available was between the nursery wall and the half-open door of my playroom. As I stood there, tearful and resentful, tracing the pattern of the wall-paper with my thumb-nail and pondering the mysteriousness of God in whose hand, I had recently learnt, 'are all the corners of the earth', the agent arrived with an elderly couple.

'This,' he announced striding across the nursery, 'is really another bedroom, and this another dressing-room,' and he pushed back the door of the play-room. Feeling some obstruction he looked behind it.

At this point S'wark came to my rescue. 'You can come out now,' she called. Shamefaced, sniffing and rather pink about the eyes, I emerged. The agent looked faintly surprised but the elderly couple smiled at S'wark and then looked reprovingly at me – obviously well-versed in this form of nursery discipline.

A day or so later a huge furniture van arrived. I remember being chivied from each roll of carpet on which I elected to sit to another by men in shirt-sleeves and white aprons trying to collect them from the main landing until finally chivied into the garden by S'wark. We were leaving the next day and I do not think I fully realised I would never see that most beautiful of gardens again. But I went solemnly round whispering sorrowful good-byes here and there, to flower beds, to the big Cedar, to the four Walnut trees. I even attempted a farewell to an outside lavatory retreating hurriedly at the sound from within of a protesting male voice as I tried to turn the door handle.

The following day with innumerable trunks and hatboxes, bags and baskets, a bicycle, a fishing rod, and a sewing machine, we left for Brighton.

*　　*　　*　　*　　*

Our first two weeks were spent in a small Private Hotel where, a few days after our arrival, I distinguished myself by nearly screaming it down. The cause – a seemingly innocuous bed-time story read me by S'wark, a chapter a night, after I was in bed. Innocuous, except apparently for

29

the closing sentence of that night's particular instalment.

'Come in, said the Goblin – and turned out the light,' read S'wark, and kissing me goodnight she followed his example and leaving the door open a crack went down to join my parents in the dining-room three floors below. Whether or not I slept and then woke I do not remember, only that, suddenly, the room was full of Goblins. Hideous, brown Goblins, with long tails forked at the ends like medieval demons. Dark as it was – there was only a thin line of light from the corridor showing down one side of the door – I knew this for a certainty . . . And they were everywhere – inside the wardrobe . . . at the back of the dressing table . . . behind the window curtains . . . under the bed . . . ! I screamed, then screamed louder . . . Now one was climbing stealthily on the bed itself . . . I screamed, screamed, screamed and screamed! After what felt like hours but can only have been a few minutes, a chambermaid came running. She switched on the light but between tears and terror I was incoherent. Leaving the door wide open she rushed off in search of my parents.

The soup of the evening was finished and the fish course being served before a message – via the head waiter – was finally conveyed. S'wark flew up six flights of stairs, my parents following. Even the elderly Manager presently arrived and stood peeping anxiously round the door . . .

I was not scolded – my distress was too real – but I was, very firmly, assured there were no Goblins, of any description, anywhere in the room, or the Hotel. My parents were urged to return to their dinner, the Manager retreated, and S'wark sat beside me until I feel asleep.

The next morning, after breakfast, the Manager called me into his office. I was afraid he was going to reprove me for screaming but to my surprise and astonishment he presented me with a box of chocolates. A small, orange-coloured box, square and deep – different from any I had ever seen. It contained four layers – it took me a long time to get over the marvel of this – *four* layers – of chocolate almonds. Normally a forbidden sweet, for once I was allowed them – doled out daily. I kept the box for a long time.

The Hotel still stands; its once immaculate white paint dirty and peeling, the whole structure enveloped in an overall air of decay. It looks as if the Goblins really might be in residence now.

*   *   *   *   *

Except that Hubert was there, staying with his grandmother, Brighton promised few attractions. To me, 'living at the sea' meant unlimited sand, paddling and bathing. I remembered only too well the week in October my mother and I had spent there two years previously. There had been pebbles instead of sand and October pronounced far too late in the year for paddling – much less bathing. It was nearing the end of September now and already some days were quite cold . . . I knew what to expect and was resigned.

Hubert and his grandmother were living in a Flat. What was a Flat? A place, apparently, where no noise must be made or the tenants above – or below – would complain; where you must put everything tidily away because there is only *one* sitting-room and not the unlimited space you have been used to . . . Hubert hated it, and so did I when I saw it. We both longed for the old life where there were no tenants and where space was unlimited.

After our fortnight at the Hotel we moved into a series of what were known as 'Rooms', the 'Lodgings' of an earlier generation usually referred to by their owners as 'Furnished Apartments'. We seemed hardly settled in at one address before we moved on to another. Whether this was due to the accommodation proving unsuitable in some way, or other tenants were due to move in I do not know. I vaguely remember a very disagreeable landlady at our first port of call where we only stayed a week but at the next where we stayed three, the cooking being very highly commended. There was also the attraction of a gentleman who came every evening, usually but not always, after I was in bed and sang songs, tragic and comic, accompanying himself on a harp. Whatever the weather he was there; only if the rain became almost torrential would he desist, hurriedly envelop his harp in a green baize cloth and retreat to the nearest bit of shelter.

His repertoire ranged from 'Annie Laurie' and 'Home Sweet Home' to the more popular songs of the day. One, an impassioned ditty urging 'a ride on a tram, tram car' was very popular, often calling forth requests for an encore from neighbouring houses. It went, as nearly as I can remember as follows:

'Come, come, *come* for a ride on the tram, tram car,
For you know how cosy the seats of a tram car are.
The view is so fine, and there's not much to pay,
You sit close together and spoon all the way,
And many a Miss will be Mrs some day
Through riding on top of the car!'

It had a catchy sort of tune and my father, who had a quick ear, took to whistling it, in and out of season. I remember asking S'wark the meaning of 'spoon' but alas, have forgotten her definition.

Regretfully leaving the highly commended cooking and the harpist behind – he had a special 'beat' and we never saw him again, we moved once more and spent about a month at another establishment. Almost all I remember of it was that the piano was in the basement – the sacred domain of the landlady and her daughter. I was just beginning what I called 'learning music' and neither S'wark nor I relished our daily half hour below stairs where a smell compounded of departed dinners and something akin to dry rot pervaded everything. There was also the disapproving – not to say hostile – audience. Perhaps it was because of the basement we left.

Our next sojourn proved to be of much longer duration but more by accident than by choice, for about ten days after we arrived I was suddenly taken ill. A doctor summoned late at night pronounced scarlet fever and immediate removal to an Isolation Hospital – a diagnosis flatly contradicted by another practitioner called in next morning for a second opinion, while confusion was worse confounded by the inability of the finally summoned M.O.H. to come to any conclusion.

Meanwhile S'wark and I were incarcerated in our not

over-large bedroom; a sheet soaked in carbolic draped over the door; only my parents permitted to enter, and my sisters whose Christmas holidays were imminent, diverted to our grandmother's in London. After about six weeks of what seemed eternity, enlivened only by visits from the kindly and jovial M.O.H. to see if I had 'peeled'; games of Ludo and 'Beggar-my-neighbour' with my mother; unwearied reading of *Brer Rabbit* by my father, I returned to more or less normal life. I was then an irritable – and doubtless irritating, child; clinging like a limpet to S'wark and furiously rejecting any ministrations on the part of my mother. The appearance of my sisters for the last few days of their holidays, bubbling over with their recent adventures in London, and experiences at their new school cheered things up considerably. I sat listening avidly to stories of boarding school life; marvelled at the specimens of 'art needlework' they presented to my mother; and heard with horror that 'almost everything is in French – except at tea-time and on Sundays'. (Though the Headmistress was English her very much younger second-in-command was French and it was very definitely 'Mademoiselle' who, as my sisters put it, 'ran everything'.)

Meanwhile a domestic storm was brewing and the day after my sisters returned to school it broke. While devoted to all three of us – possibly for that very reason – my mother was easily moved to jealousy. Like most of her generation she was never able to grasp that however much a child might, consciously or unconsciously, disemble, it was the nannie or the nursery governess who, if she mattered at all, mattered more than the mother. She could not see that good-mornings and good-nights, family lunches and even very frequent visits to the nursery were no substitute for one to whose permanent and reassuring presence round the clock one turned instinctively in times of stress. During my illness I had become very dependent on S'wark; now I could hardly bear her out of my sight. A similar situation had arisen early in the previous year, S'wark having devotedly nursed me through a bad attack of German Measles. My mother who was genuinely fond of her – they were to remain friends all their lives – at this particular time was not at all well and this together with our impending domestic upheaval and the recent anxiety over measles, combined to unleash a flood of jealousy. S'wark was accused of 'stealing my affection'. There was nothing for it – she must go . . . But by the time we had all three saved up for a 'parting present' my mother had regretted her outburst. S'wark was reprieved and the 'parting present', which she kept all her life, sat serenely on her dressing-table. Now things had flared up again; the same accusation was made; my affection was being stolen; and fuel was added to the flames by my mother's insistance she was now quite well enough to look after me herself, and that 'with all this dreadful education business' we should be economising more; S'wark must go. This time there was no reprieve. S'wark left.

*   *   *   *   *

Early in the first week of February, complete with the boxes, bags and bicycle, the fishing rod and sewing machine, we set forth for Falmouth; the Cornish climate being reputed to be warm and sunny at this time of year. Our stay there was scheduled for three weeks, after which we were to take up residence in Bath, in the Rooms temporarily vacant but normally inhabited by my grandmother. Though she always stayed with us once or twice a year I do not remember my 'Grannie in Bath', as I always called her to distinguish her from 'Grannie in London', very well. She was very old, and though fairly active always walked with a stick for she was nearly blind. She had lost the sight of one eye many years before, and the sight of the other was failing. To me she appeared incredibly old and her memory seemed to go back into the mists of time, recalling such historic events as voyages in sailing ships, the abolition of slavery, and incidents of the Crimean war. She had married late in life, and when left a widow many years before had lived with her son in the family home in Ireland. When he married she came over to England with her Irish – very Irish – Companion, one Miss Joyce. They settled in Bath, but every spring when my grandmother's small annuity would allow it, they set forth in the R.M.S.S. *Tagus* for the West Indies. The name of the ship is fixed for ever in my mind for I had been given one of its sailor's cap ribbons. I was very proud of this and sometimes wore it across my chest pretending I was the ship's Captain – happily unaware such adornments were only for the seamen.

My grandmother had been born in the West Indies whence her mother and two aunts – intrepid daughters of an Orcadian manse, had set forth to found a school for girls in Barbados where they had relatives. Her mother, my great-grandmother, had married there, but her husband had not lived long and, her own health deteriorating she decided to return home. Her eldest sister, fortunately as things turned out, sailed with her to help look after my grandmother – then aged four. The dramatic story of this particular voyage, remembered with such startling clarity by her, together with her memories of weeping slaves imploring not to be freed but to remain with the family, and her various anecdotes of the Crimean war were family sagas. Told, and re-told, on long winter evenings in Ireland to her own sons and daughters, they had been remembered by them with almost oriental fidelity and in due course passed on to their children. I remember looking at the bent and nearly blind old lady and trying to imagine the small indignant child helping to defy the sailors 'near mutiny', or being clung to by weeping and despairing slaves. In old age she would insist she remembered these slavery scenes, but it was her mother's not her own memories she was recalling. She herself was not born at the time of the Abolition (the Abolition of Slavery in British possessions came in 1833, some thirty years ahead of the USA). Later memories of being petted by and playing with one time slaves, now paid servants in the household, were true enough. Confirmation of them in letters written to her in later years by an old man once a family slave still exists. Of the Crimean memories, mostly of Miss Nightingale and her ladies, which my mother would relate with great fidelity, I remember only the constant mention of terrifying cold, but the weeping slaves and the dramatic story of the long journey to England remain as vivid as when I first heard them.

The voyage was made in a sailing ship. The weather in the Atlantic was very bad, and she took well over six weeks to reach her destination – Liverpool. During the last few days the food gave out, and there was nothing to eat for passengers and crew alike but ships biscuits 'many of them *maggoty*!' This item was always related with great solemnity – so that one shuddered at the mere thought of the maggots. Ill before she started, my great-grandmother had become worse as the voyage progressed, and not long before the food crisis she died. The crew, superstitious like most sailors, insisted the dead body should not be allowed to remain on board, 'but your Great-Aunt Matilda' we were told, also with great solemnity, 'firmly insisted that it should'.

Argument became very heated; there were unseemly oaths – and *threats*. Mutiny, we were given to understand was almost ready to break out ... But Great-Aunt Matilda displaying true Orcadian stubbornness, and stoutly supported and encouraged by her four-year-old-niece, stood firm. Eventually a compromise was reached. The coffin, with the remains of my great-grandmother was slung over the ship's stern and then lashed fast to the rails. There it remained until Liverpool was finally reached, when it was unlashed and taken ashore for burial.

My grandmother lived to be very old. She left us all large sums of money she had not got, and various possessions mostly belonging to her son in Ireland. My own legacy when I eventually received it, was a rather moth-eaten grey squirrel 'tippet' and muff.

* * * * *

I remember only two things about the long journey to Falmouth. We travelled on the Cornish Riviera Express – non-stop to Plymouth. Just after the train roared through Reading my mother suddenly sat bolt upright and exclaimed in anguish, 'My purse! My purse! I must have left it in the bedroom!' I too sat bolt upright, and probably open-mouthed and popeyed, for the purse was a very treasured possession. Actually it was a small bag, what was known as a 'chain-mesh' purse, made of silver. It had been given to my mother in Edwardian days when this fashion was at the height of its popularity and I knew she cherished it very much. Now nearly in tears and questioned by my father, she remembered locking it in the dressing-table drawer (we had spent the night at the Great Western Hotel in Paddington) unlocking the drawer next morning and taking the purse out; it must have been left on the dressing-table itself . . .

My father went in search of the guard, who returned with him, miraculously armed with a telegraph form. A telegram to the Hotel was written out with a description of the purse and our address in Falmouth. Together with the necessary cash this was handed over to the guard, who assured us it would be 'thrown out' at the next station and immediately despatched. And sure enough, clutching my father's hand and watching through the corridor windows as we hurtled through Hungerford at terrific speed – thrown out it was; rolled up in a sort of ball and deftly caught by a porter on the platform. And it must have been 'immediately despatched' for the next day the purse arrived safely by registered post! Today one thinks almost with awe of such magnificent organisation; the unquestioned and obliging co-operation – the honesty! . . .

The other memory is of our arrival at Truro where we had to change. It was now late in the afternoon and very cold on the platform after the warm train. The short February daylight was fading quickly and by the time our numerous pieces of luggage had been piled up beside the waiting-room door, the sky suddenly darkened and a snowflake or two fell. My parents called to me to come inside but I had sat myself down on the sewing-machine and begged to be allowed to stay and watch the snow fall. I so seldom saw any and adored it – as I still do. It came down slowly at first in large, lightly floating flakes; then more quickly and the flakes much smaller. Then, quite suddenly, it became a miniature blizzard, snow whirling first this way, then that. I was pulled inside the waiting-room and stood watching entranced through the window until the snow blurred all the panes. By the time our train was due the sky had lightened and the snow had stopped but the sewing-machine and the rest of the luggage looked like huge white-iced cakes.

A bitter wind was now blowing and the porter as he

collected the luggage remarked comfortingly he had never known it so cold – and more to follow he shouldn't wonder . . . The Cornish Riviera hardly seemed to be living up to its reputation.

The porter was not far wrong. It was, I believe, one of the coldest winters Cornwall had known for years. The 'Rooms' – recommended by some friends of my parents, also proved unsatisfactory. They were very small and dark and the landlady none too obliging. On arrival we had tea at which saffron buns predominated, and shortly after my mother began to make preparations for putting me to bed. There was hardly room to turn round in the bath-room and to her horror, for she had never seen, much less used, one, a geyser for heating the water. I remember her enveloped in a butcher-blue apron patterned with small white flowers, the bath having been filled after much grumbling by the landlady, attempting to bath me and being overcome by one of the violent headaches to which she was subject – erroneously diagnosed as neuralgia and which were responsible for the greyish-white streak in the front of her thick dark hair . . . I think my father finished the bathing; he certainly looked after me during most of our visit, my mother being prostrated by headaches and the intense cold.

The Rooms were in the centre of the town and it was – or seemed – quite a long walk to what was called 'The Promenade'. This, to me, meant sea and sand and I looked forward eagerly to both as my father and I set off to walk there. Even in the sheltered narrow streets there was a terrific wind but as we approached the Promenade itself something like a force ten gale was blowing. Brighton had its share of storms and waves were reputed to break over the Front, but I had not seen them and this was my first experience of a really rough sea. It was nearly high-tide and coming in quickly. A seething, surging sheet of water torn with jagged white-crested waves stretched as far as the horizon. Huge breakers crashed against the wall of the promenade, sending up showers of spray fifteen to twenty feet high.

Normally drawn as by a magnet to any sand, for once I

was intimidated. I stood tightly clutching my father's hand looking with something like terror at the rapidly diminishing yellow-brown strip that was briefly revealed every time the waves drained back before making a fresh onslaught. We stood watching until the last vestige of it vanished. Soon after, a particularly violent shower of spray fell rather too near and my father decreed we must return home while still dry.

On the whole I remember little of Falmouth: only narrow streets; many small shops filled with saffron buns; a long steep flight of steps known as Jacob's Ladder; a boat trip over to Flushing where Primroses were reputed to be in flower at this time of year but in the biting cold had prudently refrained . . . One thing, however, will remain associated in my memories of the town for ever – Copy Books! They were purchased by my father with, I suspect, the dual purpose of furthering my education and of keeping me quiet. They were called 'Civil Service Copy Books' though from what, if any, branch of that establishment, ranging as it then did from the humblest Post Office to the most exalted Ministry in Whitehall, I do not know. They had depressing dark grey covers; the 'copies' themselves were all smug little maxims, 'Look before you leap', 'All is not gold that glitters', and the actual letters more slanting than those to which I was accustomed. I hated them and to this day the words Civil Service have a repellent sound to me.

After a week of the dark cheerless rooms, the geyser, and a surfeit of saffron buns, we left, spent some days at a small Hotel and finally arrived at Bath rather earlier than arranged.

I think my grandmother and her Miss Joyce must have moved to the nearby Hotel so that we might have their Rooms earlier. I remember them coming in and out and my grandmother seated at the sitting-room piano playing and singing with great verve, 'Up wi' the bonnets of Bonnie Dundee!'

The day before she left for Barbados she presented me with a doll. Its clothes, she announced impressively as she handed it to me, had 'all been made by a Lunatic'. Scissors, she explained were not allowed and everything had had to be cut out with a piece of glass! Even to me this seemed a strangely dangerous substitute, and, the unforgivable sin, all the clothes had been sewn on which meant the doll could not be dressed or undressed. I rather recoiled from it anyway and it sat languishing on a chair in a dark corner of the sitting room. It was always referred to as The Lunatic Doll.

Burnet Roses – Part 3

How soon my mother regretted her dismissal of S'wark she did not reveal. But it cannot have been very long. The Rooms were comfortable, the cooking good, and though the land-lady herself, a grim-looking old lady, seldom emerged from her basement domain, her daughter – even grimmer looking – made it quite clear she did not approve of this sub-letting arrangement. We were constantly informed that 'Mrs W and Miss J' – as she always referred to my grandmother and her Companion – never did, asked for, or wanted, this, that and the other . . .

While we were at Brighton my father had begun house-hunting activities, bicycling miles, whatever the weather, to view various eldorados recommended by house agents. He would describe the more possible of these residences when he came home and I would draw what I imagined they looked like. Now he began to search further afield, sometimes bicycling sixty or seventy miles and was often away most of the day. My mother and I, left alone, were constantly at loggerheads; I resenting everything she did for me, she, not surprisingly, resenting the resentment. Because I had made little fuss at the time of S'wark's departure, I think both my parents assumed I had 'got over it' as the saying was. What was not realised was the vulnerability of a young child to grief; its limited power of expression; the time-factor – '. . . days that were as long as twenty days are now . . .'. After the first night of stunned misery spent at the Great Western Hotel, there was the distraction of Falmouth; later of my Grandmother's visits. Now, cooped up as we were, the weather damp or foggy interspersed with rain, misery took over.

S'wark wrote to me – as she had promised she would. I do not remember her actual parting with my mother but it must have been what Victorian novelists would have described as 'cordial' for she wrote to her too. As I could not read more than a few words, even of S'wark's particularly clear writing her letters were read to me, but I kept them beside my bed and many nights after the light was put out I cried for her. But I cried silently – under the bedclothes; I did not want anyone to hear, to know . . .

I am not sure but I think I wrote back – under my mother's guidance; the sort of 'thank you' letter one wrote after Christmas or birthday gifts. But I do remember that one day, engulfed in misery and longing, writing on a little slip of paper the words 'I love you' and, unseen, slipping it under the not very firmly stuck-down flap of an envelope with a letter my mother had just written to S'wark. It was a cri-de-coeur and S'wark knew, as she told me in later years, sorrowfully – and helplessly, that it was.

For the benefit of my health – ironically as it turned out – and to give me the company of other children, my parents enrolled me for two hours twice a week at the gymnasium of an establishment almost opposite us. It was of foreign origin, called, I think, The Zanda Institute. The children all wore moss-green gym tunics over tussore silk blouses and I felt very conspicuous in my blue jumper and skirt and encountered stares of varying degrees of hostility. I was also without gym shoes and this apparently barred me from what was evidently the pièce-de-rèsistance for the younger-children – climbing in and out of a large square ladder-like object called I believe a 'climbing frame'. I regarded it and its mostly rather diffident climbers with some contempt. Gym shoes or not I indignantly launched an attack on it and had got about half way up when I was forcibly removed and rebuked in a torrent of broken English by the lady in charge.

The only other activities permitted me – marching in a line with a book on my head, or doing arm exercises – 'stretch oop', 'stretch oot', 'stretch doo-an' – were not inspiring and I was not sorry when my mother called to fetch me.

But this first appearance was also my last. Before the next

session I had succumbed to 'flu – with which, though it had not been revealed, half the 'Institute' was away – and my mother followed my example the next day.

My Grandmother's doctor was away, but the landlady recommended her own who lived just round the corner. The grim-faced daughter produced hot milk and a revolting form of nourishment called 'beef-tea' at intervals and occasionally threw in a kindly word; even so we felt sure 'Mrs W and Miss J' had never done anything so inconsiderate. My father abandoned his house-hunting and spent his time doing the necessary shopping and filling hot water bottles and, the worst over, re-reading *Brer Rabbit* to me and bits from the daily paper to my mother.

Fortunately it was a mild type of 'flu and we were soon up, but it left its usual lack of energy and depression. Learning I had no-one to play with the doctor very kindly invited me to tea with his own children. His two little girls were about my age and we played quite happily together until their brothers – aged about eight and nine – returned from school. After tea, under the supervision of an elderly governess, we embarked on hide and seek. Attempting to open a door leading to the basement which I thought would be a good place to hide, I was suddenly set on by the elder boy, my hair violently pulled, and my hands grasping the door handle roughly smacked. As I continued to hold on he seized one of my wrists and quite badly twisted it. Hearing scuffles and cries the elderly governess appeared and a few minutes later my father arrived to fetch me home. I departed to jeering laughter from the boys and rather scared looks on the faces of their sisters. I was not asked again; anyway the proverbial wild horses would not have got me there. My wrist hurt for quite a long time.

My mother recovered more slowly than I did. She must, I am sure, have longed for S'wark but was not I think prepared to ask her if she would – or could – return. Instead she compromised. Highly recommended by someone, a daily governess was engaged for me.

Why Miss Barnett had ever elected to look after, or to teach children is one of life's mysteries. Few women can have had less aptitude for the job. She had neither the remotest understanding of children or the faintest capacity for teaching. It was my mother's wish that I should learn the Twenty-third Psalm of which she was very fond. I was quite familiar with Biblical and Prayer Book language and had learnt the greater part of the Church of England Catechism without much difficulty though I do remember at a later period being bogged down in what we called 'the Desire' and being refused leave to 'go on to the Sacraments' until word perfect.

But under Miss Barnett's instruction the Twenty-third Psalm defeated me completely. Though we 'had it' every morning of the interminable month she remained with us, except for the first three or four lines I was no nearer knowing it than when we started. Nor did I make any progress in reading and spelling in both of which I was already sadly deficient.

On the stroke of eleven-thirty, wet or fine, we set out for a walk, returning sharp at twelve-forty-five when Miss Barnett took her leave for the day. Her idea of a walk was to some given point – and straight back; no stopping to look at anything of special interest, no answering of questions – indeed no conversation at all. Only abrupt commands not to 'loiter' or 'lag behind'. Short of having me on a lead she might have been exercising a dog. There were only three walks in what might be called her repertoire. Fortunately the big Victoria Park was her favourite and even though one was frequently exhorted to come along and not loiter, it was by far the best.

It was now early March; fine, sunny and warm. After the long cold winter the trees were budding rapidly, making up for lost time, some leaves already beginning to unfold. Here and there a few short-stalked daisies and a celandine or two that had escaped the mowing machine showed in the sacred turf behind the 'Keep Off the Grass' notices. I was thrilled with these pointing both out with joy. But they evoked no response from Miss Barnett; only a command to 'come along quickly and stop lagging behind'.

One entrance in and out of the Park was by a small lane –

almost a path – that led past the back gardens of some houses. Since we were last there, in crevices and at the base of the garden walls, celandines had come out in quite large numbers. Their glossy petals glittering in the sun looked almost as if enamelled. I was enchanted for they were – and still are – one of my favourite flowers. It seemed eternity since I had picked any flowers – certainly wild ones. I picked as many as I could holding them up to Miss Barnett for admiration. But to her they were just 'weeds', most certainly nothing to pick and bring home in triumph. I vaguely remember her telling me to throw them away; refusing, and reporting the proposed sacrilege when we arrived home; my mother putting them in water and Miss Barnett departing looking affronted.

I think my parents must have realised fairly soon that Miss Barnett was not the paragon they had been led to expect and this episode brought matters to a head. My Grandmother would be back in about a couple of weeks, another move was ahead of us and it probably seemed a good moment to dispense with Miss Barnett's services. It must have been now that my mother, aware that S'wark's present job was soon to end as the children she was teaching were shortly going away to boarding schools, wrote to ask her if she would come back to us?

Less than three weeks later we had moved; Miss Barnett had vanished – we never saw her again; my sisters returned from school, and 'Mrs W and Miss J' were installed once more on their home ground, busily unpacking and distributing to us and numerous friends their usual cargo of shell necklaces and bracelets, 'Made by Poor Whites, my dears', my Grandmother would explain, 'One must help them.' Obviously one must, but wished they need not dye their wares such hideous blues and purples.

Our new Rooms, owned by a delightful ex-butler and his wife at the other side of the town, were a great success, the kind and cheerful atmosphere a pleasant change. But everything was eclipsed by the news that S'wark was coming back! The long misery was over; in a week – ten days – twelve days – she would be with us again!

From somewhere – possibly from the ex-butler – I had acquired a copy of the Flag Alphabet. The gaily coloured little shapes each representing a letter of the alphabet fascinated me. I decided to try to learn them by heart. It did not take very long; after the Twenty-Third Psalm they were easy going! The younger of my sisters became interested in them too. She also had an idea – 'a surprise' for S'wark, and we spent much time cutting out and correctly colouring six inch paper shapes to form the words 'Welcome Back To S'wark'. Three sets were completed, threaded on string and hung about the room she was to share with me. Over the bed; across the dressing table; between the windows. But before this activity started – actually two days after her return from school, my elder sister appeared at breakfast with her face a mass of small red spots from forehead to chin. She said they 'itched a bit' but she felt perfectly well.

'Chicken-pox,' pronounced my Grandmother's doctor, now returned from his holiday, who my mother had insisted on calling in, and he added cheerfully, 'The other two will probably have it by tomorrow.' We had; both of us felt tired and had slight headaches, but unlike our sister hardly any spots. On our mother's insistence we stayed a day in bed and one or two more what was called 'resting' while our father read *King Solomon's Mines* aloud to us. Most of it was above my head, but I remember well the gathering excitement of the last chapters and my half joy, half terror, at the horrifying dénouement when 'the door of solid rock' came down and 'Gagool' met her just deserts – squashed flat beneath it!

Chicken-pox is a highly infectious disease with a long quarantine period. I remember no quarantine of any kind and can only suppose we were all such slight cases that it was considered unnecessary. Anyway, I am sure no quarantine would have kept us, about a week later from going to the station to meet S'wark. The three of us walked there alone, returning with her and her well-remembered luggage in a cab; four ecstatically happy people.

The kindly ex-butler and his wife were unable to 'accommodate' us as they expressed it for more than three weeks as their Rooms were already let for the next couple of months. We knew that our landlady in North Devon, where we were to spend the summer, could not have us before the end of May so 'accommodation' for four weeks had to be found somewhere. I remember little of the Rooms eventually found except that they were in Bath, available for two weeks only, and had a shortage of bedrooms. The last was overcome by my father. He was taking my sisters back to school in about ten days, so took them to spend the intervening time with his mother in London, returning in time for the next move. This, which I remember well, was also for two weeks. It was to Dawlish in South Devon and I think was chosen partly because it was relatively near our destination in the north of the county, and partly because my parents had friends in the area and could combine it with a long deferred visit which included an excursion up the Dart.

The 'accommodation' was quite near the railway line and the great excitement of the day was to see the Cornish Riviera Express go thundering by and try to read the name of the engine. Usually, just as we were about to sit down to lunch, we would hear the train's approaching roar. This was a signal to rush to the window and in seconds the great green engine with its glittering brass name plate and trail of coaches would have flashed past. 'Lode Star'? 'Lone Star?' There was a long argument between S'wark and my father every time this particular engine went by, he maintaining the former, she the latter. The question remained unanswered until, quite unexpectedly, we came face to face with the said engine standing stationary at Exeter station. I added it to my list of engine names. I loved railway engines. I knew nothing, and cared less for their mechanism. It was their shapes, their sheer shining *bulk* that drew me; there was something about them which suggested a huge, powerful animal – a little frightening but very endearing. Even the names of the railway companies had a certain allure; Great Western; Great Northern; Midland; London, Brighton and South Coast . . . Coloured picture post-cards of their respective engines were distributed all round my bedroom.

The weather was perfect, the spring at its height. My

parents departed on their 'Excursion' and S'wark and I went for long walks in the narrow high hedged little lanes at the back of the town. Many wild flowers that had been over when we reached our North Devon paradise last year were still in flower. Primroses, long-stalked, their leaves grown coarse, Dog Violets, Stitch-wort – always known to us as 'Star of Bethlehem' – some Bluebells beginning to seed, and the biggest, pinkest pink Campions I have ever seen anywhere to this day. Once we got lost in the little lanes. It was getting near my bedtime and S'wark decided to take a short cut along the edge of a field up for hay. I was small for my age but even so it was amazing to find the lush grass – a good two weeks off normal cutting time – rising well above my head. *Grass – taller than oneself!* It left an ineradicable impression . . .

My parents returned from their 'Excursion' extolling the Dart and its surroundings, my mother going so far as to place it above Killarney which from an Irishwoman was praise indeed! It seemed to have been an altogether idyllic trip. They often spoke of it in later years.

Burnet Roses – Part 4

Our North Devon landlady, in her curt but kindly way, welcomed us as surely as the Burnet Roses. The long summer by the sea had begun . . .

It was a surprise, and a happy one, to find other Rooms in the house were let to a family. A mother – not long widowed, with two children – a girl of ten and a boy of five – and an ancient family retainer known as 'Nan'. They were friendly, intelligent children and in spite of the gaps between our ages we got on very well together,·though there were times when Angela seemed almost grown up and James a baby. A daily governess, Miss Stewart, bicycled six miles five days a week from the nearest town, arriving every morning on the stroke of nine to teach them. James was released after an hour, S'wark and I wrestled with the three-Rs till eleven, but Angela was incarcerated until Miss Stewart took her leave at twelve. Then, arms waving, long fair hair flying she would rush down to join us on the beach, 'Like a bard,' as Nan called it, and never failed to remark, 'released from its cage!'

I think the father of the family had not long died. Anyway his widow was entirely clothed in black except for a small white collar that rather reminded one of a parson. On Sundays, Angela, bare-legged all the week, wore black stockings, a black sash around her white dress and a black ribbon round her straw hat while James was subjected to a black arm-band. Nan, whose real name was Mrs Forbes – though whether widowed or of Brevet rank was never revealed – also wore black. This matter of mourning and the importance her generation attached to it, was reflected in a story my mother would tell of a friend, living in the depths of the country who, hearing of the death of Edward the Seventh, sent a telegram to her dressmaker in London as to the correct wear, receiving in reply two stark words, 'Absolute Black'. Mrs Kennedy was evidently passing out of the more acute stage, for by midsummer she was wearing white blouses, and soon touches of purple and mauve began to appear.

Except for morning lessons and the weather our days were governed largely by the tides. Only at the scheduled 'spring' ones or a storm – rare in summer – would the sea come more than three-quarters of the way up the big sandy crescent of the Bay. When this happened we went for walks; up the incredibly steep and narrow lanes; along the sandhills; sometimes to a dark little fir wood that reminded one of so many of Grimm's Fairy Tales.

Every morning, between ten and eleven o'clock the two rival 'Donkey Women', as they were called, would arrive. Each had her quota of five or six donkeys, two or three ponies, and a cohort of boy attendants. The boys, ranging in age from about twelve to sixteen, were mostly bare-footed, wore ragged coats or shirts and long trousers of a species of corduroy that smelt abominably in hot weather.

A corner formed by the end of the sandhills and the beginning of the rocks was the Donkey Women's undisputed – and smelly – domain. Here from their arrival until close on sunset they were in fierce competition. Both wore black dresses and white aprons. Mrs Watson, the more benign-looking of the two, seldom wore a coat but always a black straw hat adorned with several black ribbon bows, while Mrs Roberts, of much fiercer mien, affected a man's straw boater secured to her head by two long and ferocious-looking hat pins, and a ragged, over-large tweed coat, obviously once the property of her husband or some other male relative. When not actively engaged with their respective animals, or reviling their boy attendants, they were shouting their – always identical – terms.

'Donkeys! Penny to the stream! Ponies tuppence! First Rocks, donkeys tuppence, ponies fourpence!'

At half past eleven my mother, S'wark, and myself would appear and make straight for a little sandy-floored cove from which the sea had sometime receded, leaving it relatively dry and not due to return for another two hours or so. Here with rugs and cushions my mother and S'wark would make themselves comfortable and embark on their interminable sewing, leaving me to dig, paddle and play about with James – Mrs Kennedy and Nan being established also with rugs and cushions, on some rocks a little higher up.

Until late July when the schools broke up we and the Kennedys almost had the beach to ourselves, except at weekends when the 'Trippers', as they were called, would appear in large numbers. The exclusive Hotel had its quota of guests, but they kept mainly to its grounds and the golf course. There were of course other Rooms and their occupants – for the most part Nannies and very young children – and a few private houses could be rented for a month or two.

At the end of June when the Universities came down, one house quite near us was occupied by the celebrated Sir Oliver Lodge and his family. A succession of young men seemed to be constantly arriving and departing. There was a tennis court and we would hear them proclaiming the score, and exuberantly shouting to each other. There also seemed to be a number of Japanese guests. They wore very gay kimonos and could be glimpsed through the thick Euonymus hedge as one passed by, lying in deck chairs under, appropriately, Japanese parasols.

On Sundays everything changed. Breakfast was later – at

49

least ours was; I think the Kennedys must have kept to their usual hour for I distinctly remember my father, trying to snatch an extra half-hour's sleep, complaining bitterly of James, who lisped slightly, ceaselessly bouncing a rubber ball up and down on the linoleum-covered landing outside his door, chanting, 'Thweetie! Breakfast's ready! Thweetie! . . .' (Thweetie being Angela).

Among other things, on Sunday civilised clothes had to be worn. After six days of bare legs and sand-shoes, socks or stockings and 'proper shoes' were misery, likewise Sunday dresses and coats. There was also the unbelievable horror of gloves! Finally arrayed there was the ten minute dusty walk uphill to the Tin Church, as it was called – and Mr Mayne.

A stone church was in process of being built but had not got very far. Meanwhile the Tin Church complete with a little steeple that housed a solitary funereal-sounding bell, served the needs of the community. It was about the size of the average village hall and built mainly of corrugated iron. On hot days – and Sundays always seemed to be hot whatever the rest of the week had been – it was almost unbearable, while a heavy shower of rain on the corrugated roof could drown the voice of the most determined singer, and sometimes even the harmonium that did duty for an organ. Mr Mayne was the Vicar. He looked healthy enough and was by no means old – even by a child's scale of values – probably about thirty-five. Whatever the cause he was apparently easily moved to irritation – even wrath. Possibly the heat and stuffiness affected his powers of concentration – particularly during his sermon. Should a child fidget or venture to whisper there would be an ominous pause and a stony stare directed at the culprit; should either offence be repeated an even longer pause, a pointing finger, and a command that reverberated round the corrugated walls, *'Take that child out!'*

Except for a hustling sound and tears there would be dead silence. All the children, and some grown-ups, turned round while Mr Mayne stood glaring till the porch door closed upon the victim then resumed what he was saying, as if nothing had happened.

I only witnessed this scene once but we were told it was by no means infrequent. We would hear the grown-ups denouncing him among themselves but to us he was always defended. James and I were terrified of him and I think Angela was too though she pretended not to be.

*   *   *   *   *

There were wet days and cloudy days but on the whole it was a fine, warm summer. After six weeks my arms and legs were coffee-coloured and my face even more freckled than usual, 'like a turkey's egg' as my mother always described it. In the years ahead she was to spend much time, money, and energy trying – unsuccessfully – to remove them; endlessly surprised – as indeed, I was, that my sisters had 'not so much as a freckle between them!'

Towards the end of July the Kennedys went away, for a fortnight to stay with friends, and their Rooms were taken by a Diocesan Bishop, his wife, and almost grown-up son and daughter. A few days later my sisters arrived from school. Lessons for me were over too and the scope of our daily doings was much enlarged.

On rainy or uncertain weather days, or the few occasions when the tide was very high leaving rocks one usually sat on well under water, and wet for many hours, we went for walks. The Burnet Rose had passed the zenith of its flowering but now and then, from late blooms, one still caught the penetrating sweetness of its scent. But most days were spent on the beach – or beaches – for besides the sandy crescent of the big Bay there were two others. One, small, sloping and entirely of shingle was known locally as the Shell Beach and much patronised by visitors for its renowned cowrie shells.

His family tried to entice the Bishop here but he was tired with his Diocesan labours and said he believed he could do as well on the landlady's shingly paths. And to everyone's amazement, clad in an old grey flannel suit he would lie for hours flat on his stomach, humming quietly to himself and leisurely rooting about in the shingle. The landlady had looked rather askance at what she evidently considered

51

undignified behaviour in a Bishop but expressed pleasure and genuine surprise when he eventually presented her with a handful of cowries and other small shells.

As the summer progressed two large bell tents advertising 'Devonshire Cream Teas' and other delicacies were erected under the cliffs at the top of the Shell Beach. These were very popular with exhausted shell-hunters, and in August 'The Trippers' swarmed like flies about them.

We had our own places for finding shells. One, christened 'Cowrie Cove', was a narrow gully in the rocks not far from the Shell Beach. At low tide it was full of small shingly pools that yielded far more treasure than we ever found there. We considered it almost private and were inclined to assume intimidating stares at any stranger who ventured to join us. A second place, known as 'The Puffing Hole' really was private – private in the sense that we never met anyone near – much less inside it.

It was a deep cavern-like hole some fifteen to twenty feet deep by about ten across. At high tide a seething, bubbling cauldron, but once the tide went out a real treasure house for shells. The shingly ground sloped upwards to where the waves had scooped out what was almost a small cave. Dozens of shells were washed in here, and dozens more were trapped, as the water drained back, in a shallow pool behind a ten-inch ridge of rock that formed a kind of fence guarding the cavern's entrance. Here, cowries, 'fans', and 'lace-steeples', as we called them, lay all unblemished and the biggest of their kind. Often there would be glorious pieces of glowing, rainbow coloured mother-of-pearl. These were greatly prized!

Access to the Puffing Hole was dangerous; a step by slippery step descent down jagged, forbidding-looking rocks, and my father had to be in charge of any expedition there. The same applied to the second beach which was also considered – and was – dangerous, and we were only allowed there if he was with us to keep a wary eye on the tide. Some of the beach was flat and sandy but the greater part consisted of narrow ridges of tall grey rocks. Between these ridges the out-going tide left deep, clear, pools; their lower surfaces were fringed with thick seaweed and behind it lurked huge shiny green-grey prawns.

I was frightened of the really deep pools in some of which I would have been out of my depth but the smaller ones yielded almost as good a catch and the water was so clear that one went boldly in, getting soaked to the waist and feeling equipped for anything with a strong Breton shrimping-net brought back from France two years ago.

The danger came from the sea, the sudden, treacherous, always unexpected turning of the tide. For while absorbed with the prawns, '. . . far out through creeks and inlets making . . .' 'the main' would very definitely have been '. . . flooding in', and the first one knew of its approach was the sudden rising of the water in a pool, and in seconds, powerful wavelets breaking against one's legs. Seawards, the sinister stretch of dark water, visible from all three beaches, could be seen more clearly; darker now and flecked with foam. This was the dreaded Morte current with all that its name implied and from which my father – as already told – had rescued a young man many years before (Convolvulus, p. 11).

*　　*　　*　　*　　*

Into this round of peaceful amusements burst Uncle Herbert, though burst was the effect rather than the manner of his appearance. Uncle Herbert was my father's uncle – my great uncle – destined, it would seem, to play a vital rôle, one way or another, in two generations, of our family. (My father's close ties in early life with him are told in another chapter – First School.) He was living now in a small market town about twenty miles away and, house-hunting abandoned for the school holidays, my father had gone over to see him.

Though North Devon as a possible 'habitat' – at that period considered by those who did not live there as the back of beyond – had never been contemplated, the subject of house-hunting must inevitably have been discussed, for a week or so later a post-card arrived at breakfast announcing that Uncle Herbert and what he called 'your *Ant* Julia' were coming over and would be with us about two-thirty 'on urgent business'.

There were groans all round for a very special picnic had been arranged for that afternoon. But even if Uncle Herbert had been on the telephone – and I think he was – there was no question of my parents putting him off for a mere picnic – especially as he evidently had something important to discuss. He had indeed! He had found the perfect house for us! A friend, the present occupier had become very ill and must move at once. There were five years of his lease to run, a tenant must be found immediately, and Uncle Herbert had been given a first refusal for us.

I remember very vividly my resentment; the picnic baskets all packed up; the sun blazing away outside as we all sat mewed up in the small, stuffy little sitting room while Uncle Herbert discoursed at length, not only on the house itself but its surroundings and neighbours.

'*Exactly* the right size – both house *and* garden . . . *Delightful* situation – only two and a half miles from the sea, and one of the finest golf courses in England! (The fact that neither of my parents played golf seemed quite immaterial.) '*Charming* neighbours; nice, retired people – Service families – Diplomatic – Indian Civil; sons – eligible young men – coming and going . . . With your daughters growing up you must think of these things!' he admonished my father, apparently oblivious his own two elder daughters – both nearing their thirties were still unattached. Eventually my parents were persuaded – or perhaps commanded would be more accurate – to come over next day and 'see the place for yourselves'.

By the time we arrived at the proposed picnic site the waves were breaking over it. 'Ant' Julia took command and decreed we should sit on the cliff above 'and enjoy the beautiful view'. A strong wind was blowing and every time the methylated spirit under the tea-kettle was lit the flame blew out. Eventually she was persuaded to descend to a more sheltered spot on the rocks below.

The picnic over, and although they had a train to catch and proposed walking the two and a half miles uphill to the station, our relatives seemed in no hurry to depart. The tide was still coming in and I realised there would be no going on the beach for me for by the time it turned it would be my bed-time. The talk going on was above my head; I had ceased to listen to it when I was suddenly aware of 'Ant' Julia's head jerking in my direction; a warning finger being held up to my mother, and the words 'Little pitchers have long ears!'

I was already wondering about an earlier remark of hers. 'So this,' she had said greeting me on arrival with a pecking sort of kiss, 'is the little Afterthought!' But pitchers with ears!

In the landlady's very neat bathroom on a shelf about a foot above the bath stood a row of enamel hot-water cans and what she always referred to as her 'pitchers'. These were jugs of varying sizes made of the reddish-brown Devon pottery. When bed-time came I stood in the bath awaiting S'wark and carefully scrutinising each pitcher in turn. All, as expected, were ear-less.

As she bathed me S'wark laughed and explained about Pitchers, and Afterthoughts. I had not, consciously, been a Little Pitcher before but now, where 'Ant' Julia was concerned, I thought perhaps in future I might be. There seemed nothing to be done about being an Afterthought . . .

The next morning my parents set off to meet Uncle Herbert and see the property in question, taking me with them. Why this was so I do not clearly remember, but think S'wark was going away for a few days and my sisters invited on some excursion with the Bishop's family.

As soon as we arrived I was despatched by the tenant's wife to play with her grandchildren. These, together with a Nannie and a great deal of paraphernalia, were installed on a rug in the shade of some elm trees bordering a tennis court. The children were about two and three years old; I was unused to very small children and my efforts at conversation met with no response at all. The Nannie asked me my name and age and I felt disapproved of me. Conversation lapsed. I sat staring at the house. It looked quite nice but there seemed to be other houses very near. Except in 'Rooms' I had never lived in a house where other people might be able to see into one's garden and did not feel I would like this, but what really mattered – and mattered above everything was the sea – always so far from us – *was only two and a half miles away*! S'wark and I could *walk* there!

What eventually decided my parents to take the house I am not sure. By now they were probably very tired of house-hunting and we could not spend the winter months where we were. A casting vote may well have been the news that my mother's elder brother-in-law, then commanding the Devonshire Regiment, was retiring and he and her sister decided to live somewhere in the south of the County. Whatever the reason, the remainder of the lease was duly signed. In two weeks Uncle Herbert's friend had moved out and as soon as some necessary papering and painting were done we were to move in.

It was now nearly mid September and very soon my sisters would be returning to school. September the 12th was a day of celebration – my eldest sister's seventeenth birthday – and a grand picnic with a grand cake from the grand newly opened 'Cafe' was arranged for the afternoon. She was expecting – and longing – to leave school soon and spent most of the morning indulging in a kind of dress-rehearsal for the wearing of grown-up clothes. First her long, straight hair, tied back with the usual black ribbon school bow, had to be 'put up'. It was thick, heavy hair and took every hair-pin my mother and S'wark combined could produce. At last, precariously fixed 'à la Pompadour', she borrowed one of S'wark's hats and, final symbol of grown-up status, a spotted net veil of my mother's. She was very pretty – and knew it and, oblivious alike to the disapproval of authority and the derisive comments of my other sister – even sometimes from myself – would spend much time gazing into her looking-glass or posing and striking attitudes.

My father who was an ardent photographer, rushed for his camera. He never missed the smallest family event. My own progress had been photographically recorded from a day old, held in the arms of the presiding nurse and, being a bitter January day, the photograph taken in the green-house. As a very small child I would voice my hostility to what I called

56

being 'hoeshied' in no uncertain terms but over the years I had become resigned.

Alas! The birthday photographs were not a wild success. Unused to a veil the wearer had tied it too tightly. She had very long eyelashes, and these, to her confusion, kept entangling themselves in it. My father waited patiently as she tried in vain to extricate them while my other sister and myself stood by convulsed with laughter. The eventual results showed a rather plain young woman; unsmiling, eyes screwed up, and looking nearer twenty-seven than seventeen!

A week or so later my sisters returned to school and very soon after the Kennedy family departed. We ourselves were to have left at the end of the month but our departure was delayed until early October as the painters were behind with their work. Actually the house was still uninhabitable when we were due to move in and as a result we had to spend five days in some rather deplorable Rooms in the town. Of these I remember two things only. One was the landlady informing us with pride, awe, and in broad Devonian, that among the nuns at the nearby French Convent, 'they'me up eighteen Titles'! The other memory is of my mother's scandalised horror when two roast chickens arrived at lunch with what I joyously wrote to my sisters 'their heds on'!

By October autumn had set in. There were blustery winds, the sea rough, tides high. For two or three days before we were due to leave my mother and S'wark were immersed in a frenzied orgy of sorting out, discarding, or packing the accumulation of nearly five months. My lessons, except for an enforced daily half-hour of hated reading, were in abeyance. On what I called The Last Day, in spite of a howling gale, my father and I were encouraged to go for a walk to get us out of the way while the last of the packing was completed, and I have never forgotten S'wark's good temper and patience at what befell us – or rather me – as a result. We went to the Shell beach, now tentless and Tripperless. I ran ahead of my father and stood waiting for him beside a tall, jagged grey rock, scene of many games and known always as 'The King's Fort'. The tide was coming in, the sea rough but still a long way from where I stood when suddenly an enormous Atlantic roller overtaking and swamping all the other waves, swirled up the shingle flinging a deluge of spray over the King's Fort and drenching me to the skin!

My father hurried me home, dripping in every direction. S'wark had just finished fitting into the trunk the last item of my clothing except the dress and coat I was to wear next day – we were making an early start – what I had on was to be packed after I had gone to bed. As it was every stitch I was wearing had to be removed and myself put in a hot bath to prevent a chill. Every garment, the sea water first washed out of it, had to be rinsed, dried, and ironed; an entire set of underwear extracted from the lower layers of the packed trunk where everything had been fitted in with the neatness and ingenuity worthy of a jigsaw puzzle. And not a word of reproach; not a gesture of impatience!

S'wark was a really miraculous packer; an asset that was to stand her in good stead when after a long, long engagement, and years after their first meeting with the Burnet Roses, her marriage to Basil was to involve her in so much foreign travel.

CHAPTER 3

Dogs

1 Scamp

ALL THROUGH MY childhood there were dogs; loved and loving; an integral part of life.

My earliest memories are really second-hand and concern Scamp, a fox-terrier belonging to my father. He may well have owned her before his marriage; she was certainly there during the early infancy of my eldest sister in London where my parents were then living, and though her death occurred during or not long before my first year so that I never consciously knew her, she was the subject of so many small but often recalled incidents that she remains a living memory to me . . . Her devotion to my father – was only equalled by her devotion to my sister to whom apparently she became a self-appointed protector sitting alertly on guard beside the cot or pram during the briefest absence of the nursery-maid; later accompanying walks, joining wary-eyed in paddling or swimming, and later still panting loyally after a bicycle. There were episodes such as that of the Irish train guard who seeing her crawl under the carriage seat at his approach and in the easy-going rural Ireland of the time convinced of the absence of a dog-ticket, smilingly remarked she was 'an illigently trained little doorg'! There were also innumerable photographs – one particularly appealing of her, proud and adoring with a litter of puppies – the very personification of maternal satisfaction.

But it was the tragedy of her death that most impressed me. My father rarely spoke of it but others, particularly if some cat or dog showed signs of enmity, would recall it. How soon after my parents moved from London to the country the original incident occurred which eventually led to the tragedy I do not know. Presumably they had kept no cat in

London but considered a country house required one.

To Scamp, as to most of her breed, cats were anathema. Though the two animals were kept as much as was possible apart, and Scamp was a very obedient dog, they sometimes met and sparred. One day Scamp – or the cat – went too far; result – the cat used its claws and Scamp lost an eye. Two or three years later the incident was repeated. Rather than allow her suffering or endure his own, her master carried his friend and devoted companion of so many years to the orchard at the back of the house and shot her.

*　　*　　*　　*　　*

I had scant contact with cats in the years immediately following this but the horror of the story had prejudiced me against them. A prejudice in no way lessened when later, staying in Devon and sitting one morning at the breakfast table, my bare legs dangling beneath it, the landlady's cat elected to sharpen its claws on them. An episode in my late teens confirmed it for ever.

'Hovering between life and death' – as a Victorian 'novelette' would probably have described it – with septi-caemia, and rather nearer death than life, a nurse left my side for less than two minutes. The door was just ajar and the Nursing Home cat, about to have kittens, streaked through it, climbed up the back of the bed and landed on my head. Galvanised into consciousness by the weight of the cat and the returning nurse's frantic mutterings as she removed it, followed by her agonised entreaties to me not to mention the matter to the surgeon, may possibly have stimulated my ebbing powers of resistance and subsequent return to life. Nevertheless, though I admire their looks I still shudder at the too-near approach of any cat.

2 Shee-ar

Only a few unconnected memories remain to me of my first, personally remembered dog. She was an Irish terrier – Sheila by name, and had been given to my eldest sister when I was about three-and-a-half by someone unknown to me.

A possible reason for this bestowal was that Shee-ar as I called her, though of impeccable pedigree had one great – and all too obvious defect. Instead of the normal ears of her breed, Shee-ar's stood starkly upright – like those of a cairn or bull-terrier's; an affliction known, I believe in canine circles as 'bat-eared'. Assurances by the giver that as she grew older the ears would become normal must, I am sure, have been received with scepticism by those in authority for Shee-ar was already about six months old. Probably rather than disappoint my sister a period of trial was agreed on.

In an attempt to encourage the bat-ears to droop naturally my father painstakingly tried gluing pennies to them – one on the inner side of each ear. Shee-ar of course bitterly resented these appendages and promptly bit or scratched them off, but he persevered for quite a long time and provided the glue held – which was not always the case – Shee-ar gradually became resigned to them. Unfortunately the fact of their existence eventually became known in the neighbourhood and on our walks abroad Shee-ar was frequently decoyed by small boys into gate-ways or back alleys and relieved of her ornaments, returning to us literally penniless and with ears as bat-like as ever. Finally the experiment was abandoned.

But apart from the bat-ears Shee-ar presented other problems. One was that she had never been really efficiently house-trained and at the end of three or four months showed small signs of improvement. It was also about this time that Gypsy appeared on the scene.

Gypsy, or Gyp as she was called, belonged to the gardener. Whether she was about to begin her daily visits to us or had begun them and there was concern for harmony between two bitches I do not know; only that for reasons never explained to me Shee-ar abruptly left us – probably to return whence she came but this I do not remember.

I do remember that my sister was not unduly upset. Unlike my other sister and myself, and in spite of Scamp's devotion in early years, she was never an ardent dog-lover. In later years it became a family joke that she would never take the then-reigning dog – at this time Tim, another Irish terrier, for a walk unless she considered he 'went' with the clothes she was wearing.

3 Gyp

As already mentioned Gypsy – or Gyp as she was called, really belonged to the gardener. He was a bachelor, and as his landlady objected to a dog on her premises when he was out, it was arranged Gyp should spend her day with us and she arrived every morning with her master, complete with her dinner ration. Sometimes she stayed a weekend, rations always provided, and sleeping happily on old sacks in the long-disused stables.

She was a huge dog – a cross between a mastiff and a brindled bull-terrier. Immensely strong – her exuberantly wagging tail would often knock me over – she had a deep, big dog's bark and on occasion a rather ominous growl. Strangers looked askance at her but in reality she was gentle and sweet-tempered; she also had the virtues of being not only house-trained but garden-trained. No lawn was ever sullied; no bones ever buried. Galloping wildly after Hubert or myself any encroachment on flower beds was always scrupulously avoided. Even on scorching summer days, rushing madly among them to dry herself after wallowing with joy in soggy wet grass under the walnut trees – sometimes caused by a leaking stand-pipe – not one bed was ever damaged.

But with all these virtues Gyp had one serious defect and one that at times could be frightening, even terrifying. Amiable with all other breeds, for some reason nobody knew, she had a hatred – amounting to a phobia – for spaniels – she had in fact killed one and badly injured others. We had been duly warned of this by her master and if she came for walks with us, as she often did, a wary watch had to be kept, and if anything remotely resembling a spaniel was sighted her curious lead – a short, thick plaited-leather affair that could also be used as a whip – was hurriedly slipped through the ring on her broad, heavily spiked collar, and a rapid about turn effected.

Fortunately, living in a town spaniels were relatively rare.

The only one we knew was an ancient, smelly, and not agreeable specimen called Bosh. Bosh lived, appa/ permanently, in the back room of a little bakery-cum/ shop – the last shop in the neighbourhood; a kind of out-post where the paving stones abruptly ended and a path of gravel-mixed-with-mud proclaimed the beginnings of a more rural area.

During our not infrequent calls at this establishment, one of us always had to remain outside with Gyp, diverting her attention away from it, and the possible but unlikely appearance of Bosh. Meanwhile inside the owner, Mrs Stafford, would be putting her invariable query concerning bars of a special French nougat for which my sisters had a weakness.

'Mont-telly-*mart*? And how many shall I put you?' and the transaction over, meticulously weighing out a penny-worth of something more digestible for me. Only once, out for a walk, with S'wark and myself was there a hint of trouble. Crossing the road in the distance was a man with what looked suspiciously like a spaniel. Gyp was busy sniffing round a way-side tree. S'wark hurriedly bent down and slipped on the whip-lead but before we could effect the necessary right about turn, Gyp looked up. She stood staring, ears back and growling faintly as if, like us, uncertain . . . Mercifully both man and spaniel – if spaniel it was – had now crossed the road and a second or so later disappeared down a side street. But S'wark was taking no chances; Gyp still on the lead we right-about turned and went home. But a walk one Sunday afternoon when my father and sisters set off to visit some friends three or four miles out in the country ended very differently.

It was winter and they set out immediately after lunch in order to come back before dark. I remember waving to them from the dining-room window as they went down the drive, Gyp who was spending the week-end with us bounding delightedly beside them at the prospect of a walk. Less than five minutes later the Sunday calm was rent with shouts and yells and terrified screaming. A minute or so later, breathless from running, the younger of my sisters burst into the dining-room.

'Pepper! Pepper! Quick!' she gasped. 'It's Gyp – she's killing a spaniel!' . . .

Luckily the table had not been cleared and grabbing two small pepper-pots she rushed away.

It was horrifyingly true. Apparently they had barely emerged from the gate, to see, too late, just ahead, a young spaniel walking sedately between its owners. In a split-second Gyp was on to it. My father rushed forward lashing blows that would have deterred any normal dog. The spaniel's master made frenzied efforts to pull Gyp away by her tail, while his wife stood by screaming hysterically. A crowd collected; someone suggested calling the police . . . But by now the pepper arrived. Shaken well over Gyp's face it was quickly effective causing her to sneeze and release her hold for a second and be pulled off her victim. Dripping with blood, alternately sneezing and growling she was dragged home by my father and another man, given a terrific thrashing and shut in the stables whence she emerged next morning without a trace of remorse and seemingly as docile as an old sheep.

The spaniel was badly injured. I am uncertain if it had to be destroyed but we took Gyp for no more walks.

I am uncertain too of what eventually happened to Gyp herself. She was not about at the time of our packing up and departure; I loved her deeply and would certainly have remembered any farewell. I was probably resigned to her absence thinking she had disappeared into that, never of course explained to me, purdah common to what were then always referred to as 'lady dogs', and took it for granted she would be with us again some day. But I have an uneasy feeling that soon after we left, the onslaught on spaniels became more frequent and finally led to her having to be destroyed. Though in early days I must often have enquired for her, this was never revealed. And strangely – because phobia or not Gyp was a loving, and delightful dog and it is with love and delight I remember her, only a confused and uncertain memory of its confirmation in later years remains.

4 Bob

The thought that I might possess a dog of my own never occurred to me until I went to stay with Effie when I was about four-and-a-half. She was my first cousin; her elder sister was away at school, her father with his regiment in India – whence his wife after one sojourn, had flatly refused ever to accompany him again – and she was living with her mother near Tunbridge Wells.

My mother and I had gone there from Brighton where she had taken me to benefit from its renowned air after very nearly succumbing to severe dysentry during the preceding summer.

We stayed while at Brighton with an old friend of her youth from Ireland, the widow of a General, who lived with a Companion in one of those beautiful houses, now almost all converted into flats, in Sussex Square. I remember nothing of the house except its magnificent curving staircase. This was indelibly impressed on me but less for its beauty than by the sight of our hostess who, though she was widowed many years and had received us the previous day in normal clothing, descended it clad from head to foot in deepest mourning and dabbing at her eyes with a black-bordered handkerchief. It was a Sunday and evidently a weekly ritual.

'You see,' the Companion in a suitably lowered voice explained to us, 'the General died on a Sunday.'

I think we stayed a week but I remember little of the visit beyond playing on a steep pebbly beach in very hot October sunshine and being furiously indignant at not being allowed to paddle. My experience of the sea-side was limited to flat sandy beaches and almost unlimited paddling and I thought Brighton a poor sort of place. My only consolation was searching for pieces of the old-time ginger-beer bottles; small, flat bits of glass of a beautiful pale emerald that 'abraded by the sea' could be found gleaming here and there among the pebbles.

My cousin Effie then aged about eleven was a most odd child; so painfully shy or reserved, that she would rush away and climb a tree, shinning up to its topmost branches at the sight of a stranger. Even more peculiar, at any reproof or criticism she would retreat upstairs and whatever the time of day undress and put herself to bed. She appeared to be receiving no education of any kind and I gathered from her in later years there was a day of reckoning when her father's regiment completed its tour of duty abroad and he returned to his self-centred wife and by then almost aboriginal young daughter.

Her mother, my Aunt Jessie, was my mother's eldest sister and from all accounts had always been considered 'difficult'. I think her apparently total lack of imagination may have been partly to blame. She most certainly had no understanding whatever of children, nor any sympathy with them.

I was put to bed soon after our arrival and she elected to bring me my supper while my mother was unpacking. It consisted of a bowl of lumpy, very badly made bread-and-milk with grapes floating in it – hardly the most suitable fare for a child recovering from serious dysentry. I did not have grapes given me at any time at home; they looked attractive – and tasted even better. I wolfed the lot – skin, pips and all while my aunt stood complacently by. Shortly after I was violently sick, all over the bed 'and the clean sheets'. The latter were seemingly what Aunt Jessie was by far the most concerned about; their fate rankled for a very long time.

Effie was almost too shy to speak, much less play with me, but she had one great asset; she owned a dog – a fox-terrier called Bob – and when she was up a tree or putting herself to bed, Bob and I played very happily together. Before our visit was over I had decided, I too would own a dog. He must be 'just like' Bob – and I would *call* him Bob . . .

I think my mother rather welcomed the idea, doubtless regarding it as an asset, 'a great amusement!' as she termed any occupation that absorbed a child's whole attention. This was always said with a faint trace of a brogue which was as rare as her occasional 'Irishisms', as we called them; the expressive 'I haven't sat down since I got up;' 'Show it till I see;' or an all-embracing and very endearing word 'fliget'. During our recent days on Brighton beach there had been 'not so much as a fliget of shade'.

*　　*　　*　　*　　*

I am not sure when I actually became a dog-owner but I think it was early in the following Spring. I was now five and evidently considered by my parents sufficiently mature to undertake the care of a pet. They had been in London and before leaving visited the Lost Dogs' Home at Battersea. Saddened by the number of forlornly yelping inmates, and almost overwhelmed by the choice, they had managed to select a young and healthy-looking fox-terrier strongly resembling Effie's Bob, and arrived home with him the same day, complete with brass-studded collar and shining steel chain.

How old Bob was when he came to us of course we did not know. Probably he was about three or four; anyway too old to instil much in the way of obedience into him; definitely 'not amenable to discipline' as the phrase went. He got on well with Gyp however and they enjoyed chasing each other about or sitting, side by side, sunning themselves on the front doormat while waiting for their morning walk – a sight which evoked my first effort at poetry.

'Cock-eyed Bob and Gypsy,
When they're on the mat they're tipsy.'

Hardly great verse; and, consciously, I had never heard the word 'tipsy' and certainly had no idea of its meaning. I have a vague memory that I made it up trying out various 'rhymes' for Gypsy. I was rather pleased with my effort and went about tunelessly humming it, wondering – and rather affronted – when grown-ups laughed.

But Bob had other lady friends beside Gyp and was constantly what was called 'running away'. Sometimes he disappeared for several days. This would greatly distress me. I was fearful he had been run over or stolen. My father began to get tired of putting notices on the front gate – even in the local paper, and handing out half-crowns to small boys who would arrive at the back door with information – once or twice with Bob himself attached to a bit of old chain or rope. Long speculation over the reason for his presence at the Battersea Dogs' Home became clearer.

Like most fox-terriers Bob was quick tempered. He

growled, often snapped, and, once, bit my arm. I forget what prompted it and it was more snap than bite. There was little blood and only the faintest trace of teeth marks were visible. But it was enough. My mother was alarmed. Next time, she declared, it might be a bad bite. Though fond of dogs she held strong views as to their behaviour and place in society. I well remember her vehement indignation on return from a visit to her old home in Ireland, at 'a dog on every chair in the drawing-room!' and her denunciation of her sister-in-law for allowing it. Bob's fate was sealed.

The crisis came at an opportune moment – not long before we were due to embark on our travels when he would probably have had to find a new owner anyway. As it was, S'wark's youngest prospective sister-in-law was longing for a dog. The business failure which was to reduce her parents to poverty, cause Basil to leave Oxford without a degree, dependent for years on badly paid school-mastering, and consequently indefinitely prolong his engagement to S'wark, had not yet occurred. Bob was received with rapture and in spite of all remained with the family to a ripe old age.

5 Puff – Part 1

'The dearest dog that ever lived,' I found scrawled in childish writing on the back of a photograph, some years ago. The object of this veneration that looked back at me from the photograph itself was a young wire-haired terrier bitch with soft velvety ears, the shining black nose of perfect health, and eyes that expressed devoted canine affection.

'Pop' as she was first called (her Kennel name had been Poppy), later to become 'Puff', had been given me not long after we finally settled in Devon – a kind of compensation for Bob who, as previously recorded, had had to be 'given away' once our travels began and had found a happy home with S'wark's youngest future sister-in-law.

Puff was far more of a play-mate than Bob had ever been. I think in our own way we each compensated the other; for me a substitute for the long-prayed-for little brother or sister who had never materialised; for her, transition from one

68

among a love-starved pack to individual attention and affection.

Of all little dogs Puff certainly had all – and more – of the virtues attributed to those paragons frequently advertised in newspaper columns under 'Household Pets'. 'Clean;' 'obedient'; 'good-tempered'; 'excellent with children' . . . Getting on for eighteen months or so when she came to us, she was not only house-trained but over the period of cutting back-teeth when the chewing-up of books, bedroom slippers, and other accessible objects can sometimes be rampant. She was not, of course, without vices but these were relatively mild. Rabbiting was one but this might be said to be in the blood. The groom-gardener of a neighbour whose property adjoined ours, also owned a wire-haired terrier – one Prince. Prince was an older dog and a confirmed rabbiter but he was pleased to have a companion – and a female one at that – for his excursions. The two became great friends and often went off rabbiting together for half a day or more, for although we were living in a town it was only a small one, our house was on the outskirts and fields, heath-land and small copses were within less than ten minutes walk.

Like most bitches, Puff was greedy and once she had attained the art of sitting up and 'begging' she practised it in, and out of season, and particularly if any visitors were present. In fact so persistent did these supplications – if such they can be called – become, that before the end of her brief life, her short little terrier's tail was beginning to spread and flatten and threatening to resemble an otter's rudder! She had a third vice – and an unusual one; at least I, personally, have never met or heard of any dog that practised it. My father grew raspberries of which he was very fond. Some grew in the garden itself but the majority, in company with some gooseberries and red and black currants were in a wire cage. Puff had no interest in either the gooseberries or the currants but to the raspberries she seemed drawn as if by a magnet. Those growing outside the cage were an easy prey but the door of the cage was, or was supposed to be, kept shut. Sometimes, however, it was left insecurely latched. By some unerring instinct she would always discover this and be found inside rapidly denuding the raspberry canes of every vestige of fruit within her reach. Likewise, if she saw anyone even approach the cage she was immediately beside them and if they went inside more often than not would somehow manage to squirm in with them and before she could be caught, start stripping the raspberry canes like a starving wolf.

So much for vices – far, far outweighed by virtues. 'Excellent with children'. Some much stronger adjective would be needed for one particular child! For nearly four years Puff and I were to be almost inseparable companions and never once in the whole of that time did I know her exhibit temper, disobedience or real unwillingness to play with me, however hot or cold the day, ridiculous the game. After S'wark left and I began to go to school she was almost always at the front gate to see me off and to greet me with rapturous joy on my return. She slept in a basket in my bedroom and during my period of nightmares (described in 'First School') showed no resentment when, having at last nerved myself to turn on the light, I would wake her, grab her collar, and my last flicker of courage fortified by her nearness, drag her, half-asleep, past the hooked back baize door, up the three stairs and along the short, narrow corridor to either my parents' or one of my sister's bedrooms. She would wait until I was safely installed, then return to her basket – and interrupted sleep.

When I was promoted to bathing myself she never failed to accompany me to the bathroom. When ablutions – which consisted less of washing than of soaking luxuriously in hot water and playing at turning the taps on and off with my abnormally long toes – were over, and I stood dripping on the bath mat, she would immediately begin to lick me dry. Starting at my feet she would continue methodically upwards as far as she could reach on all fours.

Authority was never told of this activity. I think I felt instinctively it would not approve. Remembering it now, it seems a strange phenomenon. Was it some innate fear of water – of drowning? Puff was no water-loving dog – rather the reverse. At the sea it took much coaxing before she would come paddling – and then only briefly. She was miserable at any attempt to pull or push her into a shallow rock-pool, or to be made to swim in a deep one. Even when a periodic bath for herself was decreed she always made frantic efforts to hide.

As I grew older I was allowed to bath her myself. Immediately she saw the tin tub used for the purpose placed on a board across the bath, and myself, sleeves rolled up and clutching a cake of red carbolic soap, she would disappear; into the garden if a door was open; under a bed; behind boxes in the box-room . . . But once in the bath, soothed with pattings and endearments, but looking more miserable every minute, she would go through the operation, occasionally licking my face to show she bore no resentment. But sometimes, in summer, released into the garden to complete her drying, she would try to get her own back. Making for the first available bit of grass she would roll and roll eventually standing upright – covered with green stripes!

She was very quick to learn. When she first came to us I had recently read, or, more accurately, had read to me, a book in which some circus dogs appeared and I was determined Puff should emulate them. The wooden hoop which I bowled with vigour in winter, played a large part in these endeavours. In no time at all Puff was jumping back and forth through it, while I held it gradually higher and higher. Laid flat on the ground it formed what I called 'a circus ring', and various doggy tricks of the period, 'shaking hands' – usually rendered 'give a paw'; begging, and the popular 'trust!' (a lump of sugar precariously balanced on the nose until the command 'Paid For!' when it was jerked in the air, neatly caught, and rapidly chewed up in anticipation of a repeat performance), often took place thus encircled. This was always so with what I called Public Performances, the public, occasionally specially invited guests but usually contemporaries who had come to play, or friends of my parents or sisters who happened to be present.

Other accomplishments were more domesticated. One was being harnessed between the shafts of a kind of dolls' push-chair – a curious object – relic I now suspect of some by-gone nursery. It was of wood, painted pale blue; two 'shop-sized' dolls (see also Toys: Part 2) could be accommodated on its chair-like seat, but the long handles studded at intervals with various hooks and rings were more like shafts and really meant to be pulled by something rather than pushed. With assorted bits of string attached to her collar Puff was 'harnessed' and would uncomplainingly walk, run – occasionally gallop – about the tennis court, with a couple of dolls wedged into the pale blue carriage seat, for quite long periods.

* * * * *

At five years old I had questioned my mother about what are now called 'the Facts of Life', and was not to be put off with the 'gooseberry bush' and other myths prevalent at the time. To begin with they cancelled each other out and, instinctively, I felt they were false. As I continued to badger her she took refuge in what might be called long-term strategy. 'I'll tell you all about it when you're twelve', she promised, and I remember counting slowly on my fingers and remarking reproachfully, '*That will be seven years to wait!*'

How was it, I have often wondered since, that one accepted strange and mysterious fairy tales unquestioningly. Was it, with them, any sneaking doubts were shelved or unheeded but that fictions about the facts of life could not be so tolerated, and that with them one instinctively demanded 'the truth, the whole truth' and knew, also instinctively, when this was being withheld?

For a time my interest waned, but when I first went to school it was temporarily re-awakened by some gratuitous, and wildly distorted information, imparted by a contemporary with whom I had made friends. With the acquisition of Puff, however, these 'obstinate questionings' came to the fore again. Occasions – infrequent it is true – arose when she must be 'shut up' in the stables. There was a strong emphasis on '*must*' and it was dinned into me that *on no account whatever* was I to leave either the door of the hitherto empty loose-box, now filled with clean straw where Puff was incarcerated, or the stable door itself unlatched. At times Puff howled and yowled and I would go in and sit with her. I was also allowed to take in her dinner and other snacks – each time the solemn warning about the doors being given.

What was it, what appalling, ghastly thing would happen should I fail to obey? I asked but got no satisfactory answers; even my sisters looked smug. 'Oh you'll know one day,' was the most I ever got from either. I also observed, putting two and two together and making five, or more. Thanks to my friend at school I was a little, but very little better, but mostly erroneously informed. Meanwhile poor Puff was getting no exercise. I could see no reason I insisted why she should not go out – *on a lead*, only to be met with an angry veto. And then, one day, go out she did.

I had been to take in her dinner – early, I think, because we were going out somewhere. I came from the loose-box leaving her happily feeding. Lost in my thoughts I pulled the door to but I suppose did not really shut it. Likewise the outer door. Ten minutes later I heard my father shouting furiously that someone had left the stables open and that Puff was nowhere to be seen. We were just about to have lunch but everything was abandoned. Searchings all over the house and garden went on, there were frenzied shouts, whistling and callings. I cried, my mother scolded; my sisters looked at me with a mixture of pity and contempt. My father went about muttering angrily.

Our field and those bordering the very long drive belonging to our neighbour formed a small sloping valley. Where his drive ended, gates opened to a short steep hill, houses on one side, sloping upwards towards a busy main road. Someone looked over this little valley to where the two roads met and it was clear that something was going on there. The something was a gathering of dogs – dogs of all breeds large and small – mainly large. Even without field-glasses it was easy to distinguish them plainly. A collie; a red-setter; a curly-coated retriever . . . Sitting on her tail, the object of this homage, was Puff; standing beside her, easily distinguishable was Prince. Prince, an eye-witness friend of my father's was to tell him later, had been there all the time and was very definitely first on the scene.

And so it must have been, for about nine weeks later, after

various, to me, inexplicable changes both in stature and an unusual reluctance to perform tricks – especially Begging, Puff gave birth to a litter of ten puppies! One was born dead but all 'featured', as the cook expressed it, Prince or Puff herself. No trace of Collie; of curly-coated Retriever; no vestige of Red-setter, only ten unmistakable little wire-haired terriers . . .

My father promptly buried the dead pup, and to my horror when I heard of it drowned seven of the litter. Of the remaining two – christened for some long-forgotten reason, Caesar and Nelson, only Nelson survived for as soon as he began to crawl it was noticed that Caesar did not use his hind legs normally. They lay, immobile, crossed one over the other. While Nelson staggered shakily on all fours, his brother propelled himself along by his front legs his little back ones dragging limply behind him. My father was afraid it was paralysis; the Vet confirmed this and poor little Caesar joined his eight brothers and sisters.

Nelson now had the field to himself. He grew rapidly into a long-legged, lanky pup, with a strident vociferous yap if left alone five minutes, and a genius for damaging nearly everything with which he came in contact. We put up with him for Puff's sake, but after a time she began to snap at him, and by the time he had grown larger than herself she had lost most of her interest in him.

Fortunately, Nelson had one great admirer; the twelve-year-old boy who sometimes brought round the milk from his mother's Dairy. The transports of joy with which he greeted the offer of Nelson as a gift were worth all, and more, of the troubles the puppy had caused.

Puff – Part 2

It was towards the middle of the Christmas holidays that the tragedy happened. I was allowed to go into the town by myself now and more often than not Puff came with me. On this particular day it was very cold and I thought it was because of this that she seemed reluctant to leave the school-room hearth-rug where she was lying in front of a glowing coal fire. I called to her – several times – and even pulled at her collar but she still seemed unwilling to move. I remember wondering briefly if she was ill – her nose was hot but this might have been due to the fire. Leaving her, I went to put on my outdoor clothes, hoping against hope it might snow. Snow was rare in that part of Devon and if it fell it seldom lay for long.

My objective was not the town itself but an establishment called The Basket Shop – a kind of outpost before one reached the main shopping area, and which besides baskets of every sort, size, and description, sold ink, string, coloured chalks, and an assortment of small toys and other miscellaneous objects. I told my mother where I was going and returned to Puff. Perhaps it was the sight of my outdoor clothes for this time she got up, though obviously reluctantly. But once outside and going down the long steep hill from our house she seemed to come along more willingly, though not at all in her usual lively way, sniffing here, sniffing there, running ahead and then back to me. Instead she came very slowly and kept close beside me all the time. It was only when my purchase at the Basket Shop was achieved, and hand on her collar, we had safely crossed the main road and begun the steep climb home, that I realised something was badly wrong. Puff walked more and more slowly – almost crawled – beside me. I talked to her encouragingly but gradually she fell behind. I went back, patted and spoke endearments to her, when suddenly to my distress she lay down on the pavement giving short little moans. After a minute or so she struggled slowly to her feet and made several unavailing attempts to be sick. I grasped her collar and tried gently to urge her forward; but she held back, moaned again and looked pleadingly at me. I tried to pick her up but she was really too heavy for me and at my clumsy attempts to clutch and lift her she moaned more loudly, the moan ending in a small but piteous sort of squeak. Frightened I put her down and looked round for help, but there was no one about. Gradually, now obviously in great pain, with stroking and coaxing she began to crawl forward with little moaning rests every few yards. At last we reached the top of

75

the hill and finally our own gate. Luckily my father was just inside replacing some loose stones on a rockery. In less than five minutes he had the car out, sent me for Puff's basket, lifted her into it and on to the seat beside him and driven off to the Vet's.

It seemed eternity before he returned – and he came without Puff. The Vet had been out but had come before long. Puff, he said must have picked up some poison . . . he would do all he could but – and this was kept from me at the time – he had little hope of saving her. My father was to come back for her early in the afternoon.

The remainder of the morning passed in a kind of blurred misery. Soon after lunch at which no one ate much and conversation was sparse, Puff was fetched back. My father carried her into the house in her basket and put her near the fire in his study. I thought she was asleep but when I bent down to stroke her she opened her eyes, half lifted a paw towards me and gave a faint little twitch of her tail, then shut her eyes again. She had been given some drug and was only half – and uneasily – asleep for every now and then she would give a convulsive sort of shiver or a faint little whine.

'Poisoned' – but how? Where? She had not been rabbiting for some time; she never strayed, and anyway people did not leave poison lying about for other people's animals to pick up – or did they?

Our next-door neighbour's groom-gardener, Mr Stevens, had a son George, a nice boy of fifteen who came to help in the garden once or twice a week, and was sometimes joined by a friend called Jimmy, a little younger. Jimmy was a member of what was then called 'The Church Lads' Brigade' which he always – and frequently – referred to as 'us trained men'. He was a very conscientious youth and I think it was probably Jimmy who revealed that Mr Stevens, 'plagued' with rats, had recently announced he was putting down poison in his hen-run for them. We had heard Prince barking a great deal which he seldom did unless tied up for some reason. It looked as if there had been a reason . . .

Mr Stevens and his family lived over his employer's stables. In a field at the back was a strip of garden and a fenced off hen-run. A narrow lane separated the property from our own. A stone wall with a thick privet hedge on top bordering the field side ended in a five-barred gate through which any determined dog could – and did – get into the field itself though not the hen-run. Puff, we knew, sometimes did this, for we had heard Mr Stevens shouting abuse and sinister threats at her. She may well have gone to see what Prince was barking about; equally possible rats may have taken the poisoned bait from the hen-run, dropping some in the field outside. We could never prove it of course but Mr Stevens was a peculiarly disagreeable man. He had a sly, shifty look and a surly manner and was quite capable of tying up his own dog but giving no warning to other dog owners that poison was about to be put down. I had always disliked him; now I smouldered inside if I thought of him and later would go out of my way – even hide – to avoid meeting him.

My sisters had been asked to a dance or party of some kind that evening; it was some distance out in the country; other friends were taking them but for some reason could not bring them back and it had been arranged my father should fetch them somewhere about midnight. Puff was sleeping less uneasily now. I sat beside her until my bedtime and she did not wake when I kissed her goodnight. I went off to bed re-assured and more or less confident she would be much better in the morning. She died not long after my father had left to fetch my sisters.

'She woke up for a minute,' my mother was to tell me later, 'looked up at me, put her paw in my hand – and just went to sleep again.'

She was to sleep in my parents' room and I had promised myself I would go there and see Puff the minute I woke. It was still dark and I was barely awake when I was aware of my father coming into my room and speaking to me. He turned on the light and sat down on the bed and from the way he drew me to him, holding me tightly in his arms and kissing the top of my head I knew something terrible had happened. After he had told me Puff was dead and laid me back on the pillow again I saw tears on his face. I had never seen a man cry – I think I believed they never did – and I remember a strange sensation. For a moment, my own grief forgotten, a sudden fierce protectiveness . . . A first stirring of maturity?

My father did his best to console me. Puff was in her basket in the stables . . . she looked as if asleep . . . there was nothing to be afraid of . . . After breakfast we would go together to see her – He would bury her in my own little bit of garden . . . He would make a lovely tombstone . . .

After a pretence at breakfast we went together to the stables. Puff lay curled up in her basket as if asleep as he had said. I bent down to stroke her but instead of the familiar soft, resilient little body, my hand met a stone-like hardness; stiff, unyielding; heart-breaking. My father had not allowed for the effects of 'rigor mortis'. The shock was terrific.

I had already cried so much I did not think it possible to cry any more, but it was. My father pulled me outside and shut the stable door; and with it a door in my life.

*　　*　　*　　*　　*

The term at my new school (First School) did not begin for another ten days or so. Very sensibly my parents decided on a complete change of scene and took me to London for a few days.

I was still more or less numbed with misery and remember little of it except very real enjoyment of a pantomime performance of *Dick Whittington*, and the disappointment of not being able to meet S'wark who was now in London looking after two children whose parents were abroad. Both children had had measles and, with S'wark, were still in quarantine so our only contact was a frustrating conversation carried on standing in a street in Chelsea with S'wark leaning out of a top floor window.

*　　*　　*　　*　　*

Some might have considered it an unpropitious time to be changing schools. In reality it was salvation. Everything, from the much earlier hour of attendance in the morning; new activities like Gym and Prep; to the absence of 'Holy Pictures', 'Statues', and not kissing one's teacher on arrival in the class-room, was so utterly different from previous

78

experience that, consciously or unconsciously, most of one's being was absorbed in re-adjusting – in 'learning the ropes'. It was an almost complete re-orientation of life . . . But Puff was not, and never would be, forgotten.

CHAPTER 4
Toys

1 Dear Dick

THE CHIEF OF these was Dear Dick. Dear Dick was a striped tabby cat some eighteen inches high made by my mother from a coloured calico 'pattern', seamed up the sides, stuffed with cotton wool, and sitting upright on a stout cardboard base. Like Walter de la Mare's 'Mopser', 'his tail it curved straight upwards, his ears stood two abreast'. He had large painted eyes and whiskers, and a delicate pink three-cornered nose.

S'wark, to my great sorrow, disliked Dear Dick from the very first moment of introduction. He was, she maintained, unhygienic – not to say smelly. This was more than probable, Dear Dick having been on active service, so to speak, for over three years, day and night. In those days 'dry-cleaning' of soft toys – or even a wash in 'Lux' seems never to have been contemplated though I doubt whether Dear Dick's cotton wool interior would have responded well to the latter remedy. The only cleansing he ever received, so far as I remember, was a very occasional rub over with a damp sponge, sparingly used lest his colours might 'run', and a gentle brush, delicately administered, for fear his stuffing might protrude through his thread-bare calico hide.

S'wark's dislike of Dear Dick was in no way lessened when he accompanied us on our walks abroad, which he frequently did, dressed in a doll's scarlet woollen jumper, the empty sleeves flapping idly by his calico sides, and a scarlet beret perched on his upstanding ears. Sitting thus attired in a doll's pram, Dear Dick (and ourselves) were the cynosure of all eyes, and sometimes the subject of ribald comments which I regarded as cries of admiration but which S'wark interpreted rather differently! Pushing the doll's pram was another bone of contention between us since I had no idea whatsoever of wheeling it straight, cheerfully bumping it into all and sundry we encountered, an especially pleasing performance after a night of heavy rain. Eventually it was decreed that since I was seemingly incapable of learning to push it straight, Dear Dick could accompany us only if carried, and (this was subtle strategy) carried by me alone. Dear Dick, beloved as he was, was apt to grow very cumbersome after a mile or so. On a hot day he became unendurable. But S'wark was adamant. He must be carried – by me – or left in a ditch; better still, left at home. And very soon he was.

Dear Dick's days, had I but known it, were numbered. An attack of measles – my measles – sealed his fate. On my recovery, the day before S'wark and I were to start for convalescence at the sea, Dear Dick was missing. He had, S'wark explained, gone for a holiday as we were about to do. Strangely, he had preferred to take his away from us and where was a secret. I was uneasy, and spent the first night I could remember without his comforting stuffiness beside me, only consoled by the thought of the wonderful time he must be having. He was to return when we did. But alas! There was no return. Dear Dick's holiday had been taken in the kitchen range!

It was the one thing for which I never quite forgave S'wark . . . But this news was not disclosed immediately for my mother, with praiseworthy effort, had laboured to make what she hoped was a convincing substitute; Dear Dick, rejuvenated after his holiday. And there it was sitting upright against the pillow on my bed when we returned. But alas! I was not deceived for an instant. To begin with the substitute was slightly smaller and though probably identical in colour and design with what Dear Dick had originally been, it was not Dear Dick as I had ever consciously known him. After listening in stony silence to some coaxing to try to persuade me otherwise, I suddenly seized the impostor by an ear and, I regret to say, flung it furiously through the open window. It was then that the truth was revealed . . .

*　　*　　*　　*　　*

Dear Dick was the father of two kittens – two calico replicas of himself, several sizes smaller, and very many degrees cleaner having joined the nursery circle some two years after their beloved Papa. They were known as 'The Barrows'.

'What are the names of your kittens?' asked a kindly but rather precise visitor not long after their arrival.

'Tabby and Kits,' I answered, promptly and proudly.

'Tabby and Kits Garnett; that is very nice,' she replied.

'Not Garnett,' I remonstrated firmly.

'Not? Then what is their other – their second name?' And she proceeded to expound the necessity and custom of surnames. Everyone who was anyone, it seemed, had one. My kittens were not to be slighted. I looked round for inspiration. The gardener was mowing the tennis court. Close beside us stood a large wheel-barrow heaped high with the fruits of his labours.

'Their name's Barrow,' I said, clutching at a straw.

'Ah; Tabby and Kits Barrow. And this, I suppose,' indicating Dear Dick, 'this is their mother, *Mrs* Barrow?'

'No.'

'No?'

'No. He's their Father.'

'I see. *Mr* Barrow.'

'*No.*'

'No?'

'*No.* He's Dear Dick.'

After this it was suggested we should go and see the garden.

2 *The Skinnus*

Though Dear Dick was the chief – and certainly the best beloved, the Skinnus was my almost earliest remembered toy – indeed almost my earliest recollection. How he came by his name – a corruption of skin-horse – the toy-shop name of the period indicating real hide – I do not know. He was, I think a passed-on toy, once the property of my sisters. A skewbald, white with light chestnut-coloured patches, he stood about two feet high on a four-wheeled wooden stand. My earliest memory of him is only a small, isolated, incident but etched indelibly into my memory. Clad in a thick white coat and brown leggings I am sitting astride his back; a rope is attached to the stand and the younger of my sisters is pulling me along. The ground is of smooth wooden planks, very sharply defined, running parallel to each other and narrowing as they stretch ahead, apparently to infinity. There are groups of people standing or walking about; a blur of white painted iron-work; some brown-varnished seats whose slatted, sloping backs resemble a roll-top desk, while rearing up at intervals are tall white pipes each ending in a huge gaping red mouth – like gigantic minims.

This incident and its setting was recently confirmed by the elder of my sisters. We were aboard the deck of a Weymouth steamer, bound for Jersey. It was early January and a few days before my second birthday.

I never had a very deep affection for the Skinnus. Unlike Dear Dick and his progeny he was cumbersome – and definitely not cuddly. I think I regarded him more as a nursery asset – useful rather than beloved; he was certainly one in amusing visiting children who would play happily with him leaving me to my own ploys, while in the early transition from soft toys to dolls he played a part in bearing them on his back or drawing them in a small cart. But gradually, over the years, he came to stand neglected in the nursery until he had a brief but brilliant come-back, to be described in a later chapter (First School).

3 Dolls – Part 1

Almost any day of the week, on the dark green leather-covered octagonal table in my father's study – though as far as I know no studies except harrassing household accounts and occasional sorties to the *Encyclopaedia Britannica* ever took place there – could be seen small corpse-like figures, the unclothed bodies of dolls. China; sawdust-stuffed with china heads and limbs; occasionally wooden and even celluloid; armless, legless, sometimes hair-less, they lay awaiting repair. They varied in size from about one to four inches long for they were dolls' house dolls – a separate species – a race apart as every doll-addict knows; something entirely different from what I and my fellow addicts called 'ordinary' dolls. These were either the average twelve to eighteen inch long toy-shop variety, or the kind known as 'life-size'. There was also a third category, too small to mix with the ordinary – much less the life-size, too large for a dolls' house, being as one small boy described it, 'not in portion'.

These outcasts were, alas, occasionally presented by well-meaning adults to whom polite thanks had to be made; they fitted in a pocket, however, and sometimes in a fit of remorse for neglect or as a belated gesture of good will to the giver, one took them for a walk.

This doll addiction did not set in until after my seventh birthday when I was presented simultaneously with two of the toy-shop variety. The dolls' house ones were to come later and prove even more of an addiction – a passionate and absorbing interest.

The two dolls in question were presented, one by my mother, who in spite of an earlier failure to convert me held firmly to the idea that all little girls liked – or should like – dolls; the other by my grandmother who probably held similar views and also assumed I was getting too big for what were called 'stuffed animals'. And on the whole she was right. Dear Dick of course was now no more but Puggy and his brother Watchouses, even the beloved Barrows were beginning to pall a little. And all, with the exception of the Barrows – comparative latecomers and perhaps more dirty than dilapidated, were showing signs of irreparable wear and tear. Puggy's little red flannel tongue remained intact but his felt body had split badly. It had been stitched up many times but was now pronounced 'unmendable'. His brother Watchouses, Neddy, a small wooden horse, could no longer be pulled smoothly along because the iron wheels of his stand had cut so deeply into the wood that he was perpetually falling over, while Scamp, the eldest of the family, was in a very parlous condition indeed. A little dog on iron wheels but with no stand, he was my oldest and earliest-remembered possession, having been presented by my mother's old governess sometime during my first year, and until supplanted by Dear Dick, my inseparable companion. I still remember the uncomfortable but comforting pressure of his iron wheels against me in my cot. Now his original coat of curly astrakhan consisted of a few forlorn blobs of wool clinging to coarse grey canvas which in turn revealed a startling magenta-coloured 'hide'. His little wheels were bent and battered and it was a very long time since he could be prevailed on to remain upright, much less be pulled along.

My mother's failure in the matter of dolls, referred to earlier, concerned one Elaine – a life-size doll she had won in a raffle at a charity bazaar. Elaine was presented to me when I was nearly four and was received with more awe than pleasure. To begin with she was well over half my own height; too heavy to lift easily and awkward to carry when you managed to do so. Though proud of her I infinitely preferred Dear Dick, Neddy and Scamp (Puggy and the Barrows had not yet made their appearance). I sensed my mother's disappointment at my lack of enthusiasm and remember a feeling of unhappiness, a vague sense of guilt and of making a pretence of playing with Elaine. But it must have been obvious my affections were elsewhere and it was not until our travels nearly three years later that Elaine really came into her own. Too large to pack, she took up quite a lot of room on the seat of a railway carriage and I remember vividly the thrill when porters, seeing only her back, would ignore me and kindly offer to 'lift the little one down'! There was not only the joy of witnessing their surprise when they did so but my implied superior status; for once *I* was the elder sister – a much appreciated rôle. A rôle destined, alas, to be denied me in real life.

For some time I had added a petition to my evening prayers to the effect that God would send me a little sister or brother. About the age of six or so I suddenly desisted. Asked why, I replied bluntly, 'it would be no use now,' and refused further information. What had happened was it had slowly dawned on me that though I would have enjoyed bossing – as my sisters bossed me, it was going to be a very long time before any little sister or brother arriving now would be much use as a playmate!

I think my addiction to small dolls really set in when I first saw my cousin Freda's imposing Victorian dolls' house inherited from *her* much older sisters. It is true I had the remains – and remains it was – of a dolls' house and some of its battered contents. Never a very magnificent affair, it had belonged to my sisters who, when small, were what my mother always referred to as 'very destructive' – which I was not.

'It's all very well for *you*,' they would retort if the subject was mentioned. 'There's only *one* of you,' an obvious – and quite unanswerable argument.

S'wark over the years had now and then tried to entice me into putting some sort of order into the chaos that remained and her very last Christmas with us had made a little bed from an old chocolate box for my stocking. It was a canopied and curtained affair with what was known as a 'valance'. Both curtains and valance were of white Broderie Anglais over green satin. I was much surprised when I drew it out of my stocking on Christmas morning for I had seen those white and green materials before. During the summer S'wark had worn a white blouse with a collar of Broderie Anglais and adorned with a green satin bow at the neck. I smelt a rat . . .

For some time now I had had strong suspicions about Father Christmas or what I persisted in calling 'Scentie Claws'. But reason was never my strong point and the responses to the requests, 'posted' up the nursery chimney were nearly always most satisfactory. Had Scentie Claws *made* the bed? Could he *sew*? I later asked S'wark. She, and the housemaid who happened to be in the room at the time, looked at each other and the housemaid suggested it was probably *Mrs* Father Christmas who was responsible. My attention was diverted to other gifts and I said no more but my suspicions greatly increased.

A few weeks before the next Christmas – my eighth – the myth was abruptly and completely shattered for me. Waiting for my mother in the grocer's one Saturday morning my attention was caught by several boxes of crackers piled up near the door. Each box had a coloured picture on the lid and the topmost depicted the bedroom of a placidly sleeping little girl. An empty stocking hung at the bed-post, and a gentleman in a dinner-jacket and a lady in evening dress, both carrying armfuls of small toys were preparing to fill it.

The dénouement was instantaneous – and complete. I said nothing to anyone however but a few days later when my mother rather brusquely announced the days of hanging up a stocking were over – I was now too old for such things, I was desolated – and wept.

The younger of my sisters took pity on me. Tiptoeing into my bedroom at about eleven o'clock on Christmas Eve with a huge 'net' stocking, always one of 'Scentie Claws' most cherished gifts, she put it at the end of my bed, and tiptoed out. I woke briefly, was aware of her being in the room but fell asleep again immediately.

Waking early next morning I felt a slight pressure on my feet and switched on the light. As I undid the stocking and revelled in its contents I remember that a sudden overwhelming affection for my sister possessed me; for her love, and for the sacrifice of her scanty and frequently – often vociferously – bewailed pocket money.

Dolls – Part 2

I think it must have been the result of seeing me suddenly absorbed with the old battered dolls' house that decided my father to make me a new one. I believe it was originally intended for a Christmas present – certainly a surprise – but as I often visited the attic which housed his big carpenter's bench and watched repairs to doors and window frames take place, garden frames and seed boxes and other horticultural and sometimes domestic objects being made, it was difficult to keep it secret. He knew well enough that to have locked the door or told me not to come in would only have aroused intense curiosity for I was a most inquisitive child.

'I think you are not only Eve by name but Eve by nature,' was once said to me in reproof during a school music lesson at which I kept looking away from the music to the glass-panelled door every time anyone passed by.

I was soon enquiring what was the object under construction in the attic. 'A wheel-barrow,' I was told and at first took no great interest in its progress but was very soon struck with its appearance. 'It's a funny looking wheel-barrow,' I remember remarking. My father made no reply and I suppose I then pestered him beyond endurance. Anyway, the secret was revealed. After that of course I could not be kept out of the attic; excitement mounting as the work progressed. I gathered that during a recent stay with his mother in London my father had visited the toy department at Harrods and inspected many 'ruinously expensive' dolls' houses and come to the conclusion he could do nearly as well and at negligible cost (actually it was three small pots of paint and a few screws and hinges!). The main structure was an old packing case about three feet wide by two feet six inches high, surmounted by a sloping roof, complete with chimney stacks and attic windows. As he warmed to the work we discussed the architectural features together. I begged for a balcony – a treasured memory of our Devon lodgings, and a 'verandah' like the one in our present house. These were duly incorporated, the ornamental railings round the balcony like the plainer ones of the verandah, the banisters of the staircase, and the fence which surrounded the front garden cut out with a fret-saw from old cigar boxes; all, like the window-frames, chimney pots, the steps up to the green front door, and the garden railings, painted white.

The house itself was divided into four rooms of equal size, and a hall with stairs leading to a landing above. Both the upstair rooms had three windows, two in front and one at the side; the landing one back and one front. Downstairs to the right of the front door was a room with two windows looking on to the verandah, while the room on the left was enlarged and enhanced by the projection which supported the balcony above forming an extension – a kind of four-windowed 'bay'.

But perhaps the greatest triumph was the way in which the house opened. Instead of the whole front, hinged at one side and fastening with a hook and staple at the other, swinging open in one piece after the usual manner of dolls' houses, it was divided into two sections, one slightly larger than the other. Each section was hinged at one side and could be opened separately the two fitting together when closed as neatly as the pieces of a jig-saw puzzle. The larger section with the verandah and the green front door with its imposing flight of white steps leading by a gravel path (made of sandpaper) to the garden gate, swung sideways to the right to reveal the hall and dining room, the stairs to the landing above, and a bedroom, while the smaller section swung left revealing a bedroom above, and below the room with the imposing 'bay' – later designated by my father 'Old B's drawing room' – 'Old B' being a neighbour from whose house he had copied it. The roof could be lifted off in one piece, disclosing space for what house-agents frequently refer to as 'roomy' attics. Outside the house was painted red to represent brick, my father painstakingly outlining each separate 'brick' in white paint; the roof, gray to represent slate, treated in the same manner, each slate being outlined in darker gray. He completed the roof and the front and sides of the house but then lost patience; the back of the house was left a plain red expanse broken only by the solitary window of the landing. Later, in London, he discovered, with considerable chagrin, that paper could be bought with miniature red-brick or gray slate patterns – specially designed for dolls' houses.

All was now completed. My mother made white spotted muslin curtains for every window. The walls were papered, the floors covered with linoleum – both items from old pattern books supplied by a kindly builder, the designs for each room being most carefully chosen and all strictly 'in 'portion'. It only remained for the house to be furnished.

The stock in hand was scanty – and curiously assorted; a few things that had escaped destruction by my sisters; Mrs Father Christmas' bed; a wardrobe and a miniature German wine flagon presented, rather grudgingly, by my cousin Freda from her superior Victorian mansion, and some oddments from Christmas crackers. Not a very impressive collection, and though Christmas presents in kind and in cash were likely, it was still only early November. There was a faint chance that if my sisters went to visit our grandmother early in the New Year my parents and I might go too, stay at an Hotel and 'do some dolls' house shopping', but I pinned few hopes on this doubtful, and to me, far distant possibility. And then, one Friday morning, a letter summoning my parents to London on urgent family business arrived. This, on grounds of expense, effectively ruled out any New Year visit. But a blessed compromise was reached; they decided to combine business with pleasure. Telegrams were sent and received; three days later they set off, taking me with them.

I remember my mother fussing about my clothes and my own anxious emptying of my money-box. The virtue of thrift was not only encouraged in the family but enforced. From seven years old, at which tender age one became eligible to open a Post Office Savings account – importantly scrawling 'Surname and Full Christian names' in a Pass Book – half of every Post Lawder, as I called them, received at Christmas or on birthdays, had to be paid into it. The other half, supplemented by occasional gifts of pennies, halfpennies, and more frequently, farthings, was put into a miniature red tin pillar-box.

As the Postal Orders were usually for half-a-crown or three shillings, rarely if ever, exceeding five, the savings were not large; and only those in the money-box might be spent ... Anxiously and laboriously I shook out through its mouth, the contents of the pillar-box; anxiously and laboriously I counted up the result. It was something between fifteen and sixteen shillings and seemed a staggering – almost princely sum!

Our destination was the Berners Hotel off Oxford Street, then very popular with country visitors to what was always referred to as 'Town'.

The journey from Devon took about six hours of which the best part of two was spent travelling the forty or so miles to Exeter as leisurely stops had to be made at six or seven small stations en route. I remember little of the journey except being concerned with an odd feeling – more discomfort than pain – that came and went, subsided completely and then began again in the tip of the middle finger of my left hand.

*　*　*　*　*

Whatever the urgency of the family business a day spent at my grandmother's apparently sufficed to settle it, though other excursions – to lunch, to tea, had also to be made. She lived with her unmarried son and daughter in West Kensington, then considered a distinctly plebeian locality. The small Victorian house had been bought very cheaply many years before by my uncle as a speculation for it was rumoured there were plans for an extension of the West Cromwell Road which would open up the district and greatly enhance the value of any property there.

Over the years he had altered and improved the house out of all recognition. On the ground floor two small rooms had been knocked into one to make a good-sized drawing room. By extending part of the basement almost the whole length of the back garden, adding french windows opening to a kind of patio on what was left, an almost palatial dining-room had been achieved, while part of the front basement had been adapted to provide a show-room for the latest of his numerous changes of livelihood – at this time the collecting and selling of antique glass. Upstairs, on the flat roof where a bath-room had been added, was what particularly appealed to me, a kind of rustic creeper-clad arbour for use on hot summer days.

But alas for the speculation! For years the rumours of the proposed road remained rumours only. Eventually plans began to be discussed, and the leases of the houses on either side happening to fall in my uncle hurriedly and optimistically, purchased both, successfully letting them but converting the top floor of one into an extension of his own house. He was in the throes of this when the 1914 war broke out. The work was somehow completed but all plans for the road were abandoned and throughout the war, its aftermath and the depression of the thirties they remained in abeyance. During this period my grandmother died, but my uncle and aunt

91

lived on in the house only abandoning it when Hitler's bombs began to fall.

During the Blitz all three houses were damaged – though not irreparably and a year or so after the war ended, my uncle now living alone in an Hotel – the sole survivor of his family, patched them up and with still no prospect of the road in sight, sold them for the proverbial song. Almost immediately after, the go-ahead for the road was given, and shortly before his death, a year or so later, its long-delayed construction began.

But at the time of which I write – indeed as I was always to know it – the locality was a maddening one to visit, involving from whatever quarter one approached it either a change of infrequent Underground trains or even more infrequent buses, the only alternative a lengthy and boring walk from Barons Court Tube. At nine years old the hours thus spent in travelling to and fro and at the house itself were a particularly frustrating and agonising, waste of time. A visit had also to be made to my aunt's studio somewhere in the jungle known as The Boltons. She was a portrait painter and at the time engaged, between sittings, in painting the ceremonial robes of some exalted patron. These were draped upon a lay figure which I was sharply cautioned not to touch before we were barely inside the door.

I was in awe – not to say fear of my aunt, and always found her alarming. She was a tall good-looking woman with a haughty, domineering manner and a large bust, to which was attached the chain of her gold-rimmed pince-nez through which, intentionally or not, she always appeared to regard me with distaste. My uncle, six foot four and as different from my father as the proverbial chalk from cheese, was equally alarming. Though I did not know it then, both had bitterly resented my appearance in the world, announcing to friends and relatives that it was 'ridiculous' of my parents to have another child! Neither had the slightest understanding of children and adhered firmly to the 'seen but not heard' school of thought.

My grandmother was of a very different disposition. Her sad and relatively short married life had left her looking and seeming far older than her years. From early middle age, exhausted by her valiant struggles, she had allowed her son and daughter almost completely to dominate her life. Though devoted to her they had come to treat her as a mere figurehead. Her opinion was never asked – or listened to seriously if she gave it. She suffered from some mild digestive complaint and even her food was subject to their commanding authority. I remember in later years during my student days in London when for her sake and my father's I endured lunch at West Kensington every Sunday, how the meal was constantly disrupted by their joint 'You've *got* to eat it, mother!' screamed across the dining room and my aunt's – when raised – peculiarly shrill voice ('Like a pea-hen's', as my mother once acidly remarked); and how my father – equally devoted to his mother, would, if present, sit silent but obviously inwardly fuming.

The old lady – for old, indeed very old, she always seemed to me, had a great sense of humour, probably derived from her Scottish-Irish parentage. She also had the gift of sympathy – so marked in my father, so lacking in his brother and sister, and in later years – and possibly at the time of which I write though I do not remember it, would surreptitiously pat my mother's hand when, as not infrequently happened, some caustic remark had been made. She heard and saw far more than she was credited with doing and I remember well one very appealing characteristic. Sitting, as always, in her arm-chair by the drawing-room window, a Library book she had probably been commanded to read open on her lap, she would first look carefully round the room to make sure she could not be overheard, then lean confidingly towards one and whisper, 'Wait till they go *out* – and I'll *tell* you something!' . . . So far as I remember she took no part in the current family business having probably been directed to amuse me. I sat beside her while she pointed out the sparrows and their behaviour, and told me about her window boxes. She was very proud of these for which my father would bring or send her plants throughout the year, and kept apologising for the present sorry state of some wilting chrysanthemums.

But we had come – at least I had – to furnish a dolls' house and the worst of these domestic distractions over we set about it.

The two nearest toy shops to our Hotel were Hamleys, then as now in Regent Street, and a small but very select one near the Marble Arch. In both the choice was overwhelming! 'Suites' of furniture in cardboard boxes each item neatly sewn in; individual 'pieces' – tables, chairs; beds, chests of drawers; there were even pianos. They had only four very out-size notes – most definitely not 'in portion' and though infinitely endearing well beyond my purchasing power. There were also innumerable miniature objects; a tiny umbrella stand with Japanese umbrellas; little china jugs and basins; a work basket with scissors – the scissors almost as big as the basket; a bird-cage with something resembling a parrot inside it; minute clocks and lamps and even more minute bedside candlesticks . . .

Unfortunately the prices for similar – even identical objects – were not always the same in both shops. I was determined to get my money's worth and for the best part of two mornings I dragged my long-suffering parents back and forth between Regent Street and the Marble Arch. Finally their patience evaporated. I was told I must make up my mind once and for all or we would return home without having bought anything. The threat had the desired effect and finally my precious savings – now augmented by a contribution of five shillings from West Kensington were spent – literally unto the uttermost farthing, a farthing then being the price of midget-sized Dutch dolls.

A few individual purchases of which I was particularly proud remain in my memory. A bed-room 'suite' – very definitely of French design which included a low bed with a wooden canopy and blue net curtains with a silver stripe; a dressing-table with a swing mirror flanked by two miniature drawers, two small and three long ones below, each adorned with a silver knob to represent a handle but all miraculously opening and shutting! There were also a bedside table and a washhand stand with what looked like marble tops. All were of very shiny, rather yellow wood – and beautifully made.

This was my most ambitious purchase and cost the staggering sum of seven shillings and six pence! Another item was a
small throne-line chair. Its head-piece, arms and cabriole
legs were of carved gilt, its seat and back painted a particularly pleasing dark olive green. I hesitated a long time over
this, desperately coveting it but intimidated by its enormous
cost – to wit, half-a-crown – and the choice of so many other
desirable objects, but finally succumbed. There was also a
dining-room table that pulled apart in the centre to reveal a
kind of shelf holding two leaves for extension. It was beautifully made but far beyond my means. Fortunately it so
intrigued my father that he bought it for me. Exhilarated I
recklessly expended six shillings on four chairs to go with it.
Definitely of Victorian descent, their red plush upholstery
with a deep fringe of red cotton round each seat enchanted
me and I visualised my dolls' house family – father, mother
and two of their children sitting on them round the table.

London excited but bewildered me. The streams of traffic;
the sinister and suffocating smell of sulpher and stale air that
greeted one on entering a Tube – and sometimes an Underground Station. The thrilling but rather frightening descent
in cage-like lifts to the trains, and the trains themselves that
emerged from mysterious little inky black tunnels to stand
panting and quivering at the platform, or rushed non-stop
through the station seeming to emit some strange force so
that one felt sucked towards them as if by a gigantic magnet.
This terrified me . . . I did not say so but clung tightly to a
parental hand as they thundered by. In contrast the moving
stairways were a joy and I could have spent all day going up
and down on them! Then there were various municipal
characters such as one never saw in the small narrow streets
at home. Commissionaires – men of enormous bulk arrayed
like field marshals in full dress, glittering with gold braid and
medals who stood outside Hotels and Restaurants; police-
men in spiked blue and silver helmets moving nonchalantly
among the seething traffic controlling it by what appeared
the mere flick or wave of a white-gloved hand; and the
crossing-sweepers in short dark blue coats and parson-like
hats turned up jauntily at one side, who swept the slimy,

liquid, grey mud from the road into slimy grey pools at the kerb-side before scooping it up into their little carts.

I was amazed – and fascinated by this mud and greatly enjoyed a story my absorption with it recalled to my father of a visit he and his brother as small boys had made to their grandmother in London. Accompanying her on a walk one morning they came to a place where the road had to be crossed. Each took a hand of the old lady who was rather short-sighted, and assuring her 'here is a nice place to cross, Grannie' led her straight into a pool of similar – and ankle-deep mud at the kerb-side. And, moral, were never invited to stay with her again! . . .

This incident was related to me on a joyfully anticipated 'bus tour of the City. We were on our own, my mother with her sister up from the country on a shopping expedition. It was a raw, bitterly cold day with more than a hint of fog about but we sat happily freezing on the open-topped deck of a bus while my father pointed out various buildings and places of interest. The Strand, Somerset House, the Law Courts, the newspaper offices of Fleet Street; Ludgate Hill and the figure of Justice on the Old Bailey, just visible through the gloom; St Paul's Cathedral and, finally, the Mansion House where we descended from our chilly perch to continue our tour on foot. There were still a few horse-drawn buses and I have never forgotten the sight as we stood waiting for the traffic of two fallen horses in the road. One was obviously badly hurt and the other making pathetic attempts to get to its feet on the slippery surface. There was a large pool of blood, much shouting, and a crowd rapidly collecting. My father hurried me away but between pity and dismay, the remainder of our tour – the Bank of England, Leadenhall Market, the Monument – even the Stock Exchange – a high-light of the expedition as the scene of my father's very early labours, was marred.

A less ill-fated expedition – and perhaps my greatest surprise, was when we all three went into a large building to see what my father called 'the Moving Pictures'. The cinema, though long since established in most places had not yet reached our small Devon town. The name was unknown to me and I did not, rather surprisingly I now think, even connect moving pictures with Magic Lantern shows with which I was familiar. Instead, the description conjured up a vision of large oil paintings in gold frames attached to a kind of screen which moved slowly past one like a giant conveyor belt. The reality – tip-up plush-covered seats in a darkened theatre and a slap-stick comedy of descending ceilings and fallings into buckets of white-wash, was a revelation – stupendous and enthralling. I could hardly be dragged away!

Meanwhile the curious feeling in my finger, first noticed on our journey from Devon, and which for a time seemed almost to have disappeared, had begun to assert itself once more. On the morning after the Moving Pictures episode, when not actively throbbing, there was a strange feeling as if the end of the finger was trying to force itself through the tip of my thick woollen glove, and what had originally been a small reddish patch had become a hard yellow lump – rapidly growing larger and yellower . . .

At lunch at my grandmother's it was observed I seemed to be having trouble with my fork. It was explained I had a sore finger – which was about all I had said of it. Commanded to display it I did so to mingled expressions of surprise, concern, and commiseration, the voices of my uncle and aunt clearly conveying – even to me – contemptuous disapproval of my mother for not recognising the condition. It was, my aunt brusquely asserted, a whitlow for which, apparently, the infallible cure was a bread-poultice, and immediately lunch was over she proceeded to concoct this nauseating – and applied practically at boiling point – far from painless remedy.

While I sat as instructed, obediently holding the afflicted hand to the opposite shoulder, surplus water meanwhile seeping uncomfortably up my sleeve, my uncle recalled a story of one, Great Aunt Etty who, as a child had been similarly afflicted and treated, and, in addition been subjected to a diet so sparse that towards the end of the day, overcome with hunger, she had removed the bread poultice and eaten it. This anecdote appeared to arouse much merriment but like Queen Victoria I was not amused. I thought Great Aunt Etty a disgusting child.

By evening, doubtless stimulated by the heat of the bread-poultice, the pain in my finger had increased alarmingly. My mother produced something that was probably aspirin before going down to the Hotel dinner. But I could not sleep and a kindly chamber-maid hearing stifled weeping through the partly closed door came in and offered consolation. She was still offering it when my parents returned from dinner. It was quickly decided to cut short our stay and we returned home next day.

Worn out with pain; four days of shopping, sight-seeing and general excitement I must have slept most of the long journey. I remember nothing of it, only arriving in darkness and pouring rain, being hustled into bed by my mother, and my father ringing up the doctor who came soon after. A brief look at my finger was enough; he pronounced it 'a very nasty whitlow indeed' and without much further warning, proceeded to lance it; (an anaesthetic for anything so trivial being never so much as contemplated at this time). The gaslight over the bed was never of the brightest. The lancing was done hurriedly – possibly clumsily. To this day the finger has a curious feeling, and a distinct list to starboard.

But the dolls' house was furnished – adequately if not fully. A few weeks later Christmas and my birthday a fortnight after, brought further contributions – including the four-note piano which my mother must have bought in the London shop while my attention was diverted elsewhere.

Some months later I began to write 'A History' of the dolls' house and its occupants but my description of one, Geoffrey, the eldest son, who had been given me dressed in something resembling the uniform of a naval cadet, as 'still at Osborne but hopping to get to Darmouth in about a year' caused such derision from my sisters and such hilarious laughter from some young naval friends to whom they repeated it, that I was discouraged. The 'History' was abandoned but the dolls' house, and its occupants, remained; a deep – and an abiding joy.

I have sometimes been asked why, among my collection of 'stuffed animals' I had no Teddy Bear. Actually I did, briefly, own two. But they had been given me at the wrong time – when my 'doll addiction' had set in and supplanted all 'stuffed animals'. Though never actively encouraged – and often forbidden – the first specimen I treated solely as a mascot and would put him sitting upright firmly wired to the water cap in the centre of the car's radiator . . . But his stay with us was short-lived; I am uncertain what eventually happened to him but I rather think my mother, always averse to his appearance on the car, and knowing I never really played with him, presented him to a small relative of the postman.

The second specimen was given me rather later, a present from my father on his return from a Territorial Camp. A fellow officer had bought a similar one for his family and apparently its prowess had charmed and delighted the whole Mess, for 'Bruin' as he was called, was no ordinary Teddy Bear but what was known as a 'clock-work' one. Larger than his predecessor, thickly padded and with sleek and very dark brown 'fur', he had noticeably long arms. These it appeared were part of his mechanism and took the place of the usual 'winding up' key provided with most mechanical toys. Instead, one simply turned one of Bruin's arms, for though padded and furry like the rest of him they were actually made of steel and attached to each other somewhere in his inside, both moving simultaneously. When fully wound up he would immediately begin to turn a series of very realistic somersaults. I think my father appreciated Bruin and his performances more than I did and while grateful to him for giving me the bear, and admiring the somersaults, I was daunted by its 'un-cuddlyness' due to the stiff mechanical arms.

But Bruin's stay with us was even briefer than that of his predecessor. One Sunday afternoon after our communal tea at which some friend of my father's was present, I was asked to clear a space near the window, wind up Bruin and start him on his usual performance. This was duly done and for a few seconds all went well then, suddenly, the stuffed and furry part of one of the arms shot from its steel frame and with such force that it went straight through the dining-room window shattering a large pane of glass . . .

What happened to poor Bruin I have forgotten only that this was his last performance with us and my last association with Teddy Bears!

CHAPTER 5

The three Rs

WHATEVER INDUCED MY mother – if only temporarily, to 'engage' as she called it, Miss Grundy, I never heard. Possibly she was desperate for someone – anyone – 'honest and respectable' as the saying then was, to replace the kind and loving Miss Starling who had suddenly had to leave us on account of some trouble at home. What this was we never heard. Though she had been with us eighteen months or more, was fond of us all and we of her, and had nursed me devotedly through serious dysentery I do not remember her really well, only that I loved her and that both of us were in floods of tears as her train steamed out of the station. Most strangely we never heard of her again, letters eventually returning marked 'gone away'. We knew she had German connections and though the German Emperor and his naval ambitions were not yet the daily topic of conversation they were so soon to become, it may have been considered prudent to return to the Fatherland.

But temporary or not, Miss Grundy was a sad mistake. The daughter of a small farmer living some eight or ten miles away, she was a solidly built young woman of about twenty, clumsy in her movements and abrupt in manner. Red faced, sandy haired, she had small piggy eyes – indeed her whole appearance was definitely rather pig-like, and the effect was further emphasised by a frequent clearing of her throat in a curiously piggish grunt. It was this, together with her appearance that had made my sisters – with the not unusual callousness of young school-girls – christen her 'The Grunter'. She was probably, I now realise, rather out of her element, nervous and probably shy, but there was no denying she was definitely both unattractive and unsympathetic to children. All three of us disliked her and though we were not openly hostile she was probably aware of it – and quite possibly of her nickname.

Miss Starling was very musical. She had certainly managed to inspire my hitherto not very enthusiastic sisters to greater efforts and I remember her smiling at the way I, not much given to keeping still for any length of time, would stand silently beside the piano for quite long periods while she played short pieces from a battered copy of my sisters' Mendelsshon's 'Album for the Young'.

Among other things she had impressed on them the absolute necessity of *daily* practising. The Grunter had instructions to see this and their school prep. was duly done; her only teaching activities were confined to instructing me in the Three R's.

'Come and play with me,' I remember badgering one of my sisters.

'I can't. I've got to practise for half an hour.'

'How long is half an hour?'

'Six times five minutes.'

I knew all about five minutes; it was an all-too-familiar unit of time . . . 'Stop fussing and I'll come in five minutes'; 'five minutes more *only*' – in reference to various enjoyable occupations; 'Start putting the toys away – bed-time in five minutes' . . .

'Look,' said my sister taking pity on me and walking over to the mantelpiece where she indicated it on the clock. 'There, *that's* five minutes; and when this big hand gets *there*, *that* will be half-an-hour! Now *shut up!*'

I don't remember what game we eventually played but it seemed a very short time before The Grunter arrived announcing 'nearly bed-time; another five minutes' . . .

But to return to the Three Rs. My aesthetic senses suffered badly from The Grunter's taste in dress. On a hot May morning she would appear dressed in a thick flannel blouse of – appropriately enough – a blue always known in our family as 'pig'; a colour something between what is described among drapers as 'Royal', and a deep turquoise. This was worn in conjunction with a yellowish tobacco brown skirt which, after the fashion of the day, reached to the ground and was 'finished' under the hem with a kind of brush-like braid to ensure protection against wear and tear. The texture of this braid always reminded me of a carpet-sweeper and there was certainly no doubt that it emulated the functions of one. My chief memory of The Grunter is of her thus clad, seated at the nursery table, a copy of one of my scarlet-backed reading books in her hand. A second copy lies in front of me, and between us, we attempt to follow the doings of one Dan, who had a pan or a bun, and who spent his time putting a cat, and sometimes a hen, on a mat. He could not, poor Dan, until almost the last pages of the book, acquire anything or follow any occupation requiring more than three letters. In consequence his activities were sadly limited: I detested him and made no effort to follow them. The name Dan too puzzled me. I knew no child – or adult for that matter – who was called by it. Had it been explained it was short for Daniel in whose adventures in the Lions' Den I delighted, I might have shown more interest.

The terrible daily ten minutes allotted to this unit of the Three Rs appeared interminable. Like Traherne's orient and immortal wheat they seemed to endure from everlasting to everlasting. The nursery was at the top of the house and sitting at the table there was little to be seen from the window but the sky and the tops of the evergreen oaks that bordered the drive, but outside gardening activities were going on; Bob and Gypsy waiting for their morning walk . . . Frequently, before the ten minutes were up, large tears would gather in my eyes. The hateful blue blouse and the equally hateful big black letters of the red-backed book would swim together. Slowly the tears would roll down the side of my nose. I would lick sideways and try to catch them – wondering always at their saltiness. But it was never any use; very soon Dan and his exploits would be very damp indeed. In a silence worse than any reproof The Grunter would repair the damage to the pages with blotting paper and next morning we would begin all over again, 'and see if we can't do better today'. But we never did. I remained a reluctant and very backward reader and did not really achieve the art with any accuracy until I was nearly nine to the frequently expressed scorn of the younger of my sisters who had read fluently at four years old.

Writing and arithmetic were another matter. Writing was a joy! Vivid in one's mind as one licked the pencil and prepared for action the letters glowed, gaily coloured. Slender crimson-lake A; rotund, grass-green B; curving, beautiful smoke-blue C . . . I think these colours may have been imprinted on my mind by the square, brick-like blocks from which, at three years old, I had learnt the Alphabet with no trouble at all. For example 'A for apple' and there, on each of the four sides of the shiny white-surfaced block was depicted a big red Capital A; a small red a; and between each a large, ruddy apple. Even today, for me the initial letter of a word colours, so to speak, the whole . . . Architect, Aniseed; Academy . . . all are a rather watered-down mixture of vermilion and crimson lake. Sometimes a strongly coloured letter – R for example was orange – might dominate part of a word – Astronomy for instance is about equally divided. (There is nothing uncommon in this phenomenon – I have often met people who share it.)

Arithmetic, later to become a numbing and almost totally incomprehensible subject to me, was also a pleasure. Figures after all were much like letters, while the learning of what I called 'my two-times table' presented little difficulty – something akin to a nursery rhyme or the verse of a hymn – though definitely *not* Shakespeare. Over Shakespeare I was nearly as obdurate as over reading – but with better reason. Learning lines of Shakespeare at five-years-old may seem a little advanced but this was not so and perhaps requires some explanation. At this period both my sisters were 'Shakespeare-mad' as my mother called it. If they were not reading one of the plays in their respective forms at school they were rehearsing another for a performance at the end of term. On most days and sometimes at weekends directly nursery tea was over they would rush for the school-room calling to me to 'Come along – *quickly*'.

The school-room – so called because used for lessons before they went to school but now dedicated to the doing of prep: and for games and various activities when school friends and others came to tea – was a largish room well suited to the rehearsal of plays. Clutching Bob by the collar to give me confidence, I would reluctantly follow them. The younger of my sisters who could memorise long passages of poetry or blank verse with no apparent effort and expected others to do the same, organised – or, more accurately, 'bossed', the proceedings, the elder one supervising scenery or 'dressing up' when these were indulged in.

One particular scene from *Twelfth Night* remains with me for ever. Though the play as a whole was explained to me I did not really understand what it was about and the fact that there were far more characters than actors so that parts had to be doubled, trebled, and occasionally quadrupled was confusing, while the occasional archaic English complicated matters still further.

Though it was carefully explained to me that I was Curio – 'a gentleman attending on the Duke' (Orsino, played by my eldest sister) something in me, more frequently than not, refused to accept this metamorphosis. Occasionally I would get it right only to be told 'You see you can do it if you want to!' – never a very encouraging form of praise. More often, however, lines that should have been spoken as follows:

Curio: 'Will you go hunt, my Lord?'
Duke: Sighing like the proverbial furnace. 'What, Curio?'
Curio: Laying arm across chest, hand more or less on heart and bowing, 'The Hart'

were rather differently rendered. Stealing my sister's lines and exchanging an exclamation for an interrogation mark, and spoken rapidly in one breath, they became: 'Will you go hunt my Lord? What Curio! The Hart.' 'What Curio' assuming a rollicking kind of 'What ho!'

But we did not have to endure The Grunter for very long. My mother had now decided to 'advertise'. Applicants were asked to send a photograph of themselves and one candidate looked so charming that my mother fell for her straight away. The fact that she lived at Clifton – a very short journey to

Bath – was an added attraction for an interview could be arranged and my mother spend the night with our grand-mother, now what she liked to call 'in residence' there. An appointment was duly made, the rendezvous being at, of all places, 'The Ladies' Waiting Room' at Bath Station.

The candidate had wisely elected to wear the clothes she had worn in the photograph. My mother was very clothes-conscious; she also had the enviable gift of always managing to look both elegantly – and expensively – dressed at incred-ibly little cost. Admiration was mutual. This, together with glowing references from two former employers, and the apparently enthusiastic reception given to photographs of all three of us, with which for some reason my mother had armed herself, and S'wark – for of course it was she – was 'engaged'. In less than a week she was to be with us!

I remember nothing of The Grunter's departure – only S'wark's arrival. I had been sent out to play in the garden. It was a glorious June day; hot, sunny and with a blue and cloudless sky. After picking a bunch of everlasting Sweet Peas I walked rather aimlessly about wondering about the unknown who was so intimately to share my life. She was to arrive about half-past twelve. Suddenly there was the sound of carriage wheels. Bob, tongue hanging out and panting with heat who had flung himself down in a patch of shade, sat up, ears pricked . . . Some minutes later my mother called to me to come in.

At the top of the stairs leading to the nursery she and the stranger were standing. I was commanded to shake hands and say 'how do you do'. Ignoring the latter I stretched out a very dirty hand. With the other, pulling him forward by his collar through which I had transferred the now sadly wilting Sweet Peas, I announced firmly, 'This is Bob. He's *my* dog!' This introduction was intended less to emphasise pride of possession – though there was probably a touch of this – than to distinguish between the ownership of Bob and that of the gardener's Gypsy.

Shortly after the sound of the front door banging announced the arrival of my sisters from school. They came tearing up the stairs; introductions took place; then another door banged as they disappeared into their bedroom to wash and tidy themselves for lunch. My mother having left us, S'wark and I did likewise or, to be more accurate, S'wark 'tidied' me and I remember vividly her washing my dirty hands and the feel of a signet ring she wore which aroused my curiosity. Presently there was the booming sound of the gong for lunch and I proudly conducted her down to the dining-room.

Lunch was a family affair regarded by my parents as far as we were concerned as a sort of training ground for table manners, and by my sisters, absorbed in school affairs, as a recording of that morning's activities. After Grace – 'For-what-we-are-about-to-receive-may-the-Lord-make-us-truly-thankful-and-relieve-the-wants-of-others' – gabbled at high speed by me, I listened intently to mysteries such as, 'I only got eight – or seven or five – out of ten' – as the case might be; or, 'Dorothy, got in front of me *again* in "Geog",' – whatever that was, but the speaker was apparently compensated by 'ten out of ten for History' and commended by her form mistress, reputed to be notoriously sparing of praise.

'Dorothy' appeared constantly in these narrations. The eldest of four daughters of a Canon at the Cathedral, she was a month or so younger than my second sister and the rivalry between them was fierce and unremitting.

While S'wark cut up my meat for me I was urged by my mother to 'drink up' my milk. Milk was always a controversial matter. I hated it, but at lunch there was at least the compensation of a silver Christening mug. The fact that it was small and therefore held less milk endeared it to me more than its appearance, though I would sometimes proudly point out to visitors the initials of my three Christian names and surname ingeniously entwined in a sort of monogram on one side.

Three days a week, as soon as they had swallowed their lunch, my sisters would rush back to school. 'So bad for their digestions', my mother would lament, though she need not have worried for both had, and continued to have, digestions like the proverbial ostrich.

The rush was the need to be in time for what was known

collectively as 'Sport'; hockey in winter, running, jumping, and other competitive items in summer. On two afternoons a week and of course on Saturdays they were at home, in summer usually in the garden practising running and jumping with friends, in winter joining in my afternoon walk. Today, a friend who lived near and was the proud possessor of a jumping-stand was bringing it for an afternoon's practice.

As soon as lunch was over they raced upstairs to their bedroom calling to me to follow them.. When I arrived, rather breathless, I was hustled into the small powdering-room off it where all plans were discussed, only very special friends admitted and where, occasionally, sweets I was not normally given were produced.

'What's she like?' was the question simultaneously hurled at me by both sisters, 'Decent?' Decent I cautiously conceded she appeared, and was handed a bit of forbidden coconut-ice with instructions 'not to split'. I understood these slang terms – mainly acquired at school though firmly discouraged by the authorities there, and we were deep in a further discussion of the newcomer when there was a knock at the bedroom door. After a short pause another, and then, as no one answered, in she walked and the next minute was knocking on the powdering-room door and asking for me. We all thought this knocking very polite. Grown-ups were not usually so considerate – they just walked in . . .

As it was such a hot day our walk was to be only a short one. Where our high garden wall, that had so intimidated S'wark earlier ended, a turning from the main road led to three or four suburban houses standing in their own grounds. I hurried S'wark past the gate of the first of these.

'*A mongoose lives in there!*' I informed her in an awed voice, and rather to her surprise. Actually I only half believed it. It had been told me at a very early age by some misguided attendant to frighten me into obedience, followed with the terrifying threat that 'he' would 'get me' if I did not obey! My only acquaintance with a mongoose was an illustration in *Little Black Mingo* where it looked harmless enough. But I was taking no chances and ever since had insisted on hurrying past that particular gateway.

A little further up the road, on the other side, a turning led to a short terrace of houses. They were built on the top of a steeply sloping bank with a narrow road separating them from their main gardens; long, narrow strips each with its own wooden gate. It was a favourite walk and we knew a family living in one of the houses. This I duly pointed out to S'wark, and, with a mixture of awe and pride at owning such acquaintances, the fact that two of the family were *twins*.

The next day – a Saturday – the nursery breakfast table was covered with letters – there was even a small parcel or two – and it turned out it was S'wark's birthday. My mother, coming in to kiss us good-morning, probably sensed she would prefer to enjoy her letters and parcels in peace and arranged to take all three of us shopping as soon as she had had her own breakfast.

Having unanimously agreed as to 'decent' we decided a birthday present must be found and after much discussion and my mother contributing to its cost, a minute glass jar of a kind fashionable on the dressing-tables of the day, was bought. Its silver top depicting Sir Joshua Reynolds' 'Angels' Heads' we thought very impressive. The recipient, as she was to tell us in later years, was both pleased and touched. She kept and cherished the little jar all her life.

*   *   *   *   *

As the youngest member of the family it was considered incumbent on me to say grace at meals. For use at dining-room lunch when guests or relatives were present, I had a special 'party' grace taught me by my father. Instead of the rather pretentious and already quoted 'For-what-we-are-about-to-receive-may-the-Lord - make - us - truly - thankful - and-relieve-the-wants-of-others', it was brief and to the point. On the command to 'say grace' I would shut my eyes, fold my hands together, and announce tersely 'Benedictus, benedicat'. Then, opening my eyes smirk smugly at the assembled company who if hearing it for the first time would look flatteringly surprised or admiring. Except, of course,

Hubert who, having come to Sunday lunch with his father and hearing it for the first time, remained as always, totally unmoved by any effort of mine to impress him. I was disappointed that this small rivalry in an unknown tongue provoked no admiration for I was filled with awe – and no little envy – at his own prowess in this respect; at what seemed me the incredible way he was able to speak alternately to us and to his accompanying Fräulein in different languages without an instant's hesitation. Neither of my parents nor S'wark spoke any German but Fräulein's '*Hu*-bert, *Hu*-bert, Haben sie vergessen!' when he failed to remove his hat on being greeted by my mother or some other social lapse, became a sort of household catch-phrase. And on hot summer afternoons when Hubert came to play the words would float like a refrain round the garden, mingling with the chirp of birds, the sound of distant traffic, and the faint, discordant notes of a bugle being practised away at the Barracks.

Hubert's parents were, I think, divorced – or what was euphemistically called 'separated'. I remember allusions to 'the little sister with the mother', and grown-ups abruptly changing the conversation and assuming the special look they gave each other when they thought children were listening to something unfit for their ears; even Hubert himself once casually remarking he had a sister 'away somewhere'. He lived with his father – a retired Army Captain, and his Alsation grandmother – hence the succession of German governesses – they never seemed to stay long. He was an exuberant and happy child exhibiting none of the strains and stresses today assumed to be inseparable from the victims of broken homes.

To me, the Captain was simply 'Hubert's father' – just another 'grown-up' – though I think not yet in my category designated 'old men'. He was probably in his early thirties. I only remember him as very tall with a kind, reddish face and yellow-reddish hair. He was, I suppose, considered good-looking and he certainly had an attractive manner. The elder of my sisters evidently thought so for one Sunday when Hubert and his father had come to lunch she was moved to take some artificial forgetmenots from my best hat and put them in a pocket of the Captain's overcoat, left on a chair in the hall.

I happened to be at the front door when he returned them next morning, handing them over to my father with a very sardonic expression and some comment I do not remember. Nor do I remember much of the sequel; the lunch-hour return from school and what we always called 'an appalling row'; only my sister weeping wildly in her bedroom and, later, my mother angrily sewing the forgetmenots back on my hat.

*   *   *   *   *

Except briefly at Brighton I was only to see Hubert once again. He had just gone to a public school and I hardly knew him. He had not only grown enormously but looked far older than his years. He was still living with his father and grandmother but the former had been involved in a very bad motor-cycle accident and was seriously crippled . . . The War was rapidly approaching its final phase: the next we heard of Hubert he had somehow managed to falsify his age and joined what was then the Royal Flying Corps. Not long before the fighting finally ended he was killed – flying over the land of his many governesses . . .

CHAPTER 6
Friends – real and imaginary

Part 1

'YOU MUST HAVE had a very lonely childhood – so many years between your sisters and yourself,' has often been said to me. But with the exception of the three months bereft of S'wark, my sisters away at school and, apart from my parents, only the uncompanionable Miss Barnett, it was only rarely and briefly the case. I lived, as it were, on three levels; that of my contemporaries, the teen-age and later adult friends of my sisters'; and friends of my parents, sometimes encountered on daily walks, at Sunday lunch or at the occasional garden-party. I remember only one other lonely period of any duration. It was during the long and exceptionally hot summer when I was four years old – the summer that for me was to culminate in acute dysentery and the subsequent convalescence with my mother at Brighton, then with Effie and her 'Bob' – and, later, the departure of the much-loved Miss Starling. Because of the heat, except for a few brief shopping expeditions, the usual twice-daily walks had been abandoned and almost all my waking hours were spent in the garden. It was long before my doll-addiction phase – even 'Puggy' and 'the Barrows' had not yet made their appearance – and my only companions were their predecessors – Scamp, whose bent wheels had even then long since ceased to function, the Skinnus and, of course, Dear Dick; a companionship that was evidently to prove inadequate during the long, hot mornings and even longer and hotter afternoons before my sisters, seen briefly at lunch, returned from school at tea-time.

On the whole it was the mornings that seemed longest and loneliest, unbroken as they now were by the usual morning walk, with its brief encounters with kindly adults, and rather longer ones with contemporaries. These were mostly little boys – there was a shortage of little girls in the neighbourhood – struggling to obey the commands of nannies or governesses to be polite and remove their large straw sailorhats. As these with their wide up-turned brims that produced a halo-like effect were always firmly anchored with resisting elastic under equally resisting chins, the operation took time. There was frequently an angry exchange of words – even tears. But the greater part of each day, except for brief snatches of conversation with my busily gardening father, even briefer ones with the gardener himself, or hurried visits from my mother and Miss Starling to make sure I was 'all right', I was alone. Alone – and yet not alone, for by way of compensation I had resuscitated three long-standing but very secret companions, and in addition created 'The Family'. Two of those resuscitated, 'Pixie' and 'Reynard' belonged to a very much earlier period – I remember conversations with them in what I would then have called my 'pram' days, for they represented my right and left foot respectively. The third character was a Mrs MacGregor. Mrs MacGregor was personified in the tassel with its faintly ballet-like appearance that terminated the nursery blind-cord – and indeed most blind-cords of the period. She, too, came from an earlier era but was to survive longer than the others, for I remember conversations with her for some time after S'wark came to us. These, silent of course, would be held if I woke too early and the hands of the clock not yet in the position I knew allowed me to talk or get up. But 'The Family' as I called them, definitely came into being at this time. None of its members were of what might be called the touchable variety. They were, of course, imaginary characters having no concrete existence; at times even to me, vague, almost nebulous. Possibly because of this I eventually made a drawing of them in coloured chalks – all four characters standing in a row, and pinned it up over my bed, resolutely refusing any information as to the identity of those portrayed.

The least 'real' of the Family were its oldest members –

Mollie and Betty – who I now think must have been faintly remembered characters from some long-forgotten story read to me, as I knew no one at this time with these names. The third member, also feminine, bore the peculiar name of Pinkcombs, which must have originated either from one of the many clothing catalogues that descended on my mother at this time, or a shopping expedition with her in search of vests. Of this expedition I remember little, only the joy of being allowed to sit perched on the counter of the underwear department of a big local shop, and my pride when the kindly assistant announced I had grown, and now required a larger size of garment than that of the one I was wearing. But there may well have been pink – and probably white – 'combs' as they were called, on display and to which, in view of the coming winter, my mother's attention – and consequently my own, was drawn.

The last member of the Family was masculine, clearly recognisable in the drawing referred to with its meticulously depicted dark blue jersey, brown shorts and hatless head; its contrast with the equally meticulous portrayal of female figures in frilled dresses and beribboned hats. His name was Udder-Dudder and from whom, where, or what it was derived remains a mystery to me to this day. I remember long, whispered conversations with him and the actual asking of advice – something accorded no other member of the Family; certainly never Pixie or Reynard; perhaps, very occasionally, Mrs MacGregor. Even Dear Dick himself was not often so honoured.

My sisters' teen-age friends tolerated my presence though I suspect I was probably considered more of a nuisance than an asset. I, on my side, regarded them with a certain amount of awe, listening intently to talk of school activities; opinions kind – and the reverse – of various school-fellows, members of the teaching staff and especially of the truly awe-inspiring old Head Mistress, who, crowned with a white lace cap, I can just remember presiding over a prize-giving or making a visit to the dancing class I was later to attend. Her very presence was apparently considered enough to deter any wrong doing . . . A story was recorded in the family of my sisters' first day at the school. The younger, then aged about eight, always an outspoken and determined girl and one to whom shyness was unknown, at morning 'Assembly' – some three-hundred girls and the entire teaching staff – the Head Mistress having announced that during the coming winter months outdoor games would not be played by the younger children, had, loudly and vehemently protested, 'But that's what we've *come* here for!' and had been effectively discouraged from further speech by a mere glance from the white-capped Head.

The teen-age friends were all girls – there was a great segregation of the sexes at this period. I remember only two boys who came often to the house – both day-boys at a local school; probably the majority of the age group were at boarding establishments, but even in holiday time there did not seem to be many.

But once we arrived in Devon things were very different. Uncle Herbert had indeed been right regarding the inhabitants. Never, surely, in so small an area can so many of what were then designated the 'Upper middle-class' have been concentrated! Among the younger residents of similar social standing, and already thick on the ground, were domiciled innumerable elderly retired members of the Diplomatic Service; senior Civil Servants; Naval officers; Army officers; members of the lower echelons of the Judiciary. In India the British Raj was at its zenith. From Calcutta to Quetta retiring veterans, almost unanimously it seemed, elected to settle in the south of England, choosing North Devon in particular as the most suitable place in which to adapt to the rigours of the English climate. Diplomats; Indian Army officers; Engineers – both Civil and Military; senior members of the élitest Indian Civil Service, there they were installed in large Victorian or early Edwardian creeper-clad houses of comfortable but mostly hideous design. Venerable memsahibs bemoaned large staffs of Indian servants and the apparent inability of English cooks to make anything edible remotely resembling curry, while their husbands played rigorous golf or 'took up' equally rigorous gardening. Others migrated to near-by villages or flourished in the surrounding countryside among what were usually referred to as 'Gentlemen Farmers', and a scattering of County families.

Within three weeks of our arrival 'calling cards' were piling up on a large china dish which, after the manner of the day, stood on a table in the hall.

Among their grown-up families, few, if any appeared to have unmarried daughters but their sons – Uncle Herbert's 'eligible young men' – were constantly coming or going. Holidaying from various professions and occupations in England; on leave from ships of the Royal Navy; from the Colonies; from various 'Protectorates' and 'Settlements', or from one of the relatively unknown islands spattered over maps of the world and underlined in red to proclaim membership of the, then, far-flung Empire. There were also undergraduates 'down' from Oxford or Cambridge (except for Edinburgh and Dublin no other Universities appeared to exist).

A few weeks before S'wark's departure to, mercifully, a relatively near-by family, the elder of my sisters had left school. She was nearly eighteen – and very pretty. Even I, not much concerned with appearances – especially family ones, was made aware of this – almost awed – on seeing her attired in a grey-blue shimmering satin evening dress for what was called her 'coming-out' – a small dance, well-chaperoned by both parents, at a friend's house. 'Eligible young men' were soon arriving to call and in the early days I confronted one – a school master whose parents lived in the same road – who had become a frequent visitor – demanding to know whether he intended to marry my sister? I remember him blushing furiously for like almost all the so-called 'eligibles' he was in no financial position to marry anyone, unless of course, the lady of his devotion, in the language of the day – or, for that matter of today and of the forseeable future – 'had money'. And that, in the accepted sense, she had not. My sister had blushed too and I was abruptly told to go back to the nursery – the incident had occurred in the drawing-room where for some reason I had strayed. Later I was subjected to tearful and furious vituperation; terrible threats should I dare repeat the enormity and finally a promise extracted that such a thing should never, *never*, happen again. I made the promise – and kept it, but became very alert to – and critical of – the attributes and motives of the various young men who in future presented themselves.

It must have been at a later date for the new Dolls' House was well established, that the elder of my brothers-in-law-to-be, on leave from his Gurkha regiment and staying with his mother in a nearby village, first came to the house. An only child, he can have had scant contact with little girls but was soon making overtures to me; showing flattering curiosity about various nursery adjuncts and developing an apparently passionate interest in the Dolls' House. All, alas, as far as my sister was concerned, to no avail. But, as S'wark was fond of quoting, 'Patience and per*seve*rance, Made a Bishop of his Reverence'. He was to propose three times and it was generally conceded that it was the sight of him emerging on crutches from the door of a Red Cross hospital in London, having nearly lost a leg at Gallipoli that finally broke down resistance.

But before this time there were other suitors and I remember particularly two brothers – the eldest and youngest of a large family living a few miles out in the country. They had a legal background and the elder was already a practising solicitor. He was some years older than my sister, a dark-haired, reddish faced man – the little I remember of him; about average height and of a stolid and rather humourless disposition. The younger brother who was still at Cambridge where he was reading Law, was a complete contrast. Short, pale, with a deep upper lip, wide humorous mouth and eyes which my mother once – and very aptly – likened to a sea-gull's. He was not only outstandingly clever (he was later to become a very eminent K.C.) but a most amusing young man. One of his lighter accomplishments – popular with both young and old, was to go to one of the then prolific London 'Musical Comedies' and be able not only to remember word for word one or more entire songs, but come back and sing and play their accompanying music entirely by ear.

Both brothers had what today would be termed 'fallen' for my sister. She liked the elder – and was probably flattered by the attention of a man so much older; but she more than liked the younger. The elder brother had the seeming advantage of being, so to speak, on the spot. But absence, it is said, makes the heart grow fonder and letters passed regularly between Cambridge and North Devon. Both brothers came often to the house – singly or together. In spring and winter to 'teas'; in summer to tennis. It must have been in late autumn, for it was day-light, not gas-light, that the dramatic scene I was to witness took place, and the participants were wearing suits, not tennis-flannels.

My official bed-time was six o'clock, though it was normally nearer seven by the time I had had a bath, eaten my milk-and-biscuits supper, and was between the sheets. I was sitting on my bed in my dressing-gown and starting to eat this evening meal when I was aware of strange noises proceeding from the hall below. The baize-covered door separating what had been the last tenant's nursery quarters, and where I slept, from the corridor with the main bedrooms was already hooked back for the night as usual. I tiptoed through and peered over the corridor banisters to behold a very strange sight; the two brothers seemingly engaged in what fairy tales and sometimes history books referred to as 'mortal conflict'. They stood facing each other, their fists clenched, scowling and speaking in low-pitched, furious-sounding voices. As I stood watching, the younger brother suddenly stepped back a pace and, muttering something I could not hear, aimed an angry blow at the elder's jaw, causing him to sway slightly then stagger back a few paces. At that moment the door opened and my father came out of his study at one side of the hall, and simultaneously my mother, accompanied by an elderly visitor, from the drawing-room on the other. I am uncertain what exactly happened next, only of scandalised expostulations from both my parents, followed by vehement reproaches and even more vehement condemnation. I crept away, fearful of being seen. A minute or so later I heard the front door bang. I tiptoed back. The brothers had gone and except for the muffled sound of voices from behind the closed drawing-room door, silence reigned. Presently the door opened, goodbyes were being said, and the elderly visitor escorted to the front door. I retreated again.

Where my sister was, both during and after the affray, I am unsure; certainly not in her bedroom which with open door was near where I had stood; even more certainly not in hall, study or drawing-room. That she knew of – even witnessed – the scene was clear from later conversations and I strongly suspect she was in a little room off the hall, which housed the telephone, and where flowers were 'arranged'. The door had opaque glass panels but in one there was a small hole through which, as I knew very well, a clear view of the hall was visible!

*　　*　　*　　*　　*

Letters continued to come from Cambridge, then from London where the writer was now what I called 'learning to be a Barrister' – a long and arduous period to be followed, when completed, by it seemed an equally, if not more, arduous period of waiting before a living could be earned – unless . . . 'Unless', of course, 'one had money'. And money was something the brilliant – and ambitious – young man had not – and, also, knew my sister had not, and something, before long he was to write and tell her he must have. (He was soon afterwards to make a lucrative – and later very unhappy – marriage – but the successful, and lucrative, career was assured.)

Fortunately the affair had not gone very far, only what my sister, anyway, thought of as 'an understanding' – and a time of waiting. But she had genuinely loved him – or thought she did . . .

One Saturday afternoon some weeks later she invited me to go for a walk with her. We went to a little quarry about a mile or so away near a small unfrequented wood where we sometimes picked primroses. She carried two small parcels. These when unwrapped revealed two packets of letters – the larger one from Cambridge, the smaller from London. With the assistance of some methylated spirit these were quickly and successfully burnt. She stood silently looking on but as she began stamping out a few remaining smouldering bits of paper, I saw that she was crying. I flung my arms round her and kissed her. I had only a vague inkling of what it all meant, but I felt sure she had loved the brilliant young man with the humorous mouth and the sea-gull-like eyes, as I too, in my way, had loved him . . .

My sister did not ask me 'not to tell' and I did not; only to my other sister, then still away at school, was the expedition and its purpose ever revealed.

*   *   *   *   *

Apart from the dramatic burning, the occasion is fixed for ever in my memory, for it marked my first introduction to the spindle-berry – *Euonymus Europeaens* to the scientifically minded. Though it grows prolifically in most southern counties, in North Devon it must have been comparatively rare. I, certainly, had never seen it before. A big bush of it was growing out of one wall of the little quarry and I was fascinated with the beautiful and unusual pink of the little hanging berries newly opened to display their vivid orange seeds. We took a branch or two home.

'Peg-wood,' said my mother – its name in Ireland – and also parts of England, and no doubt she thought it had been the main object of our walk.

*   *   *   *   *

My other sister was, as I have written, still at school, but expected to leave shortly. Unlike the elder one who could not leave soon enough she had begged – implored – not only to be allowed to stay on but to go Oxford and her head-mistress had written in support and strongly urging it . . . 'An extremely able and talented girl . . . There was some deficiency in maths . . . a little coaching would be necessary . . .'

Some deficiency in maths was a nice understatement, as in almost every member of the family and running through more than one generation, it was not so much a deficiency as a non-existent faculty, and had the whole project not been strangled at birth, so to speak, maths, not my mother might well have been the deciding factor in its fulfilment. As it was, with her views on education which have been frequently mentioned, the very thought of a daughter preparing for, much less at Oxford, can only be imagined. My father, rather surprisingly, was also against it, apparently forgetting the successful outcome of his sister's career – often so ferociously opposed by his brother and himself, and the many battles she had fought – and won – to achieve it . . . That question of nude models during her second year at the Kensington School of Art (now the Royal College of Art). Both brothers were appalled! But it was nude models or no a Diploma, and since a Diploma was a kind of passport to the professional Art world of the period – especially if one expected to earn a living – consent was grudgingly given. But the final step – study at Julien's in Paris . . . Paris! . . . *Alone!* Both brothers, their ideas probably founded on a mixture of *Trilby* and other novels of Bohemian life, were adamant. It was Paris *only* if chaperoned. And for six months – a year – or whatever it was, my aunt attended Julien's, living with her mother in lodgings in one of the more respectable areas of the Latin Quarter and except for going to and fro from the studio I doubt whether she ever went anywhere – certainly to no form of entertainment – unless, in the words of the old song, 'her mother came too.'

My sister had undoubtedly heard of these struggles and she too fought hard. Her head-mistress wrote again, even more strongly, stressing her pupil's ability and even going so far as to say that with improved maths, there was the possibility of a Bursary – even a Scholarship. She also added, probably in reply to some objection, that 'Higher Education' for girls was becoming commonplace.

Alas, the phrase 'Higher Education' triggered off the memory of an incident – never indeed forgotten by either parent – concerning a young woman always referred to as 'that hoyden, Katie', and not only strengthened their opposition but definitely decided the issue.

Katie was Uncle Herbert's second daughter. She was a clever girl and in later years well ahead of her time in her advocacy for 'Women's Rights', and, from all accounts, at odds with her mother, the prim and precise 'Ant Julia', from childhood. Probably for the sake of peace she was sent to that pioneer of advanced female education, Cheltenham Ladies' College. While there, some years before I was born, but at the same house, she was spending a few days of the summer holidays with my parents. Out in the garden and hearing the booming brass gong being beaten to announce lunch, instead of entering decorously by the front door, she had vaulted lightly through the open dining-room window – a performance 'so unladylike', 'so hoydenish' that it had shocked both parents and served to confirm for ever my mother's opinion of Higher Education for girls.

*   *   *   *   *

The aspirant for Oxford left school and by way of compensation was allowed to have 'French Conversation' lessons at The Convent. I was thrilled, for once I *and* a sister were going to school together! But the thrill was short-lived. The conversation lessons were with a nun not on the teaching staff. She had been ill and some months later she died. My sister was left to fill in the boredom of her days as best she could until, as my parents probably said in the parlance of the day, she should 'marry and settle down'.

Though nice-looking, she was not pretty in the accepted sense – certainly not as her sister was. But they were very devoted and the fact that most young men were less attracted to herself caused no jealousy though she would sometimes laugh at her sister for pandering to their likes and dislikes – 'soothing their ruffled feelings' as she expressed it. Always outspoken herself she was determined to make no concessions to masculine whims or to any form of male superiority, brusquely dismissing any attempts at being 'talked down to' and firmly discouraging what she thought insincerity in any form – especially flirtatiousness. But a day came when this strategy – if strategy it could be called – failed. At a small dance given by newly acquainted friends of my parents, she met a young Naval Surgeon on leave from his ship. He was very good looking, did not talk down to her, appeared to share many of her interests, and during their last dance together invited her to meet him on his next leave at a well-known night-club in London.

Night-clubs, anyway in the country at that time, and however respectable, were considered completely beyond the pale – spoken of almost in whispers – hence their allure. My parents would have been horrified at the very idea and would never have given their consent to such a meeting place. Consequently they were not told of the invitation but S'wark's youngest sister, formerly a Sister at Queen Charlotte's Hospital, and recently married, and who was considered even by S'wark to have rather advanced views on behaviour, knew all about night-clubs. A few days in London were going to be necessary. My sister had stayed with her before and a visit to her flat at the appointed time was duly arranged.

But the 'Leave' was not yet. Meanwhile, having elected to continue teaching me my Catechism from the point where S'wark had left off, on Sunday afternoons we would repair to her bedroom where the latter part of the Catechism, as then set forth in the Book of Common Prayer, would be dinned into me. If I responded well – which was by no means always, by way of reward she would talk to me of the young man in question and produce his photograph, taken in full ceremonial dress, which she had coloured and kept in a chest of drawers, hidden away among her underclothes, pointing out to me among the wide gold stripes on his sleeve the narrow red one that denoted his status as a Naval Surgeon. I was duly impressed and longed for the day the engagement would be announced.

But there was no engagement. To say that he treated her abominably would be to put it mildly and she took a long, long time to get over the affair. De mortuis . . . Suffice it to say, neither my elder sister nor myself shed any tears when his name appeared in the casualty list of those lost at the Battle of Jutland.

My interest in the Navy, already sparked off, was not, as it well might have been, shaken by this episode. The original spark had been ignited, so to speak, on a visit to my Aunt Jessie. Her husband, his overseas spells of duty completed, had now retired and they were living, literally, on the very edge of Dartmoor. It was late in the summer holidays and I had been invited to spend a week with them. Effie, who had at last been sent to school was not there, she was staying, I think, with relatives, but her sister – older even than mine, was at home. There was also a young nephew of my Uncle's in all the glory of his first leave since promotion from Midshipman to Sub-Lieutenant – though still addressed by all as 'Snotty'.

Attired in my best 'Sunday' dress and coat, equipped with a small suitcase, a packet of ham sandwiches, four bananas and a plethora of 'do's' and 'don't's' I was allowed to travel alone to Exeter. Here I was met and driven to what I later began to think of as Paradise.

Only two things marred my visit. Aunt Jessie's introduction to my bedroom – a small attic-like apartment all by itself at the top of the house – 'I've put you in the so-called "haunted room"', she announced, opening the door, 'though no one's ever seen anything yet'; and the discovery that my mother had 'let down' the hems of the two cotton dresses and a skirt packed in my suitcase.

Aunt Jessie's remark caused me such terror that I hardly slept at all my first night. My Uncle, who I was meeting for the first time, and who turned out to be a most delightful person, soon discovered this – and the reason. For the rest of my stay my bedroom door was left open at night, and for further reassurance, that of 'Snotty's' immediately below. This greatly, if not entirely, allayed my fears. The clothes were another matter. Ahead of her time, my mother liked children's skirts to be short – two inches or so above the knee instead of the then prevailing two or three below it. For some reason she must have thought I had grown more than I had; but she had overdone it. Whichever of the three garments I wore they flapped irritatingly half-way down my legs and I hated them – passionately. This was particularly the case when wading about in the numerous little streams that trickled around wherever we went. To me these were one of the glories of the visit and highlighted by the fact that no-one said they were too cold, or too deep, or too swiftly flowing for the sailing of paper boats, nor appeared to mind if one *was* cold, muddy, wet or even downright soaking! Snotty – whose name I discovered to be Cecil, was an expert both at making and sailing these boats, very obviously enjoying it and doubtless considering me a good excuse for so childish an occupation. I for my part regarded him with awe, and listened eagerly – and seriously – to details of life at sea; especially to the many and arduous responsibilities of a Sub-Lieutenant! Before the end of the week I was well and truly 'hooked' on all things naval.

With the exception of Aunt Jessie, who always managed to avoid anything she did not like by excusing herself on the grounds of what she called 'household matters', everyone else seemed to prefer what are sometimes referred to as 'the great outdoors' or 'the wide open spaces' and, judging from the array of Burberry's, sou'westers, galoshes, gum-boots and shooting-sticks in a passage off the hall, in any and every kind of weather.

Dartmoor itself – anyway this part of it – seemed to fit the above descriptions. The miles and miles of sheer empty space! The absence of any human habitation – indeed habitation of any kind; of any animals . . . Just acres and acres of squishy rush-filled bog and boulders, or dry, springy turf, and, everywhere, swift or gently flowing streams, broadening here and there to form small still pools shaded by a tangle of overhanging bushes. Trout lurked in some of these pools and the highlight of my visit was the catching by my cousin of a good sized specimen; the making of a fire and cooking it, dangling on a string tied to another stretched between two walking sticks, and consuming it – half raw – with some hunks of bread-and-butter – Aunt Jessie's idea of 'lunch' – the whole washed down with bottles of very fizzy ginger-beer produced by Snotty with an almost conjurer-like technique from his various pockets.

On the last afternoon of my visit Aunt Jessie had to do some shopping connected with her 'household matters' and took me with her on the short train journey to Plymouth. On arrival she presented me with sixpence 'to buy a toy'. The shopping over, instead of tea in a Tea Shop as I had hoped, she purchased two sticky buns; these we consumed on the journey back.

To what original source this curious inhibition, this reluctance to spend money – often even on necessities, was due I have no idea. Both my mother and her younger sister, like many Irish people, were generous to a fault. Once, when cars had become more or less commonplace, my mother had asked her sister why, when living in so isolated an area, she and my uncle didn't buy one. To which the reply, delivered in Aunt Jessie's very slow, deliberate speech, which gave the impression that all her words began with capital letters, was, '*Maud! It Might Decrease The Balance!*' To which my mother, momentarily nonplussed had retorted, 'You can't take it with you!'

My Uncle kept his own counsel. What he thought we never knew. He had his well-earned Army pension and went his way quietly enjoying various country pursuits.

But in spite of knowing her sister's parsimonious ways, my mother was nevertheless incensed when on returning home I handed over the remnant of the lunch given me to eat in the train; some very sticky jam sandwiches and two of the four bananas with which I had set out, now nearly black!

Part 2

'Hooked' as I was, my interest in all things Naval was further stimulated, but at a rather later date, by a magazine story – so stimulated indeed that for some months I literally 'became' a Naval Officer. The fact that the story in question concerned the Merchant, not the Royal Navy, mattered not at all! It was originally published in a children's magazine called *Chatterbox* which appeared, I think, weekly and with what publishers used to refer to as 'profuse illustrations'. Near Christmas-time the whole of the year's instalments would be bound together in the form of a large, thick Annual. One of these volumes, always a year or more out of date, would arrive as a combined birthday and Christmas present from my Uncle's wife in Ireland whom I had never seen.

I was, as already mentioned, an extremely backward

reader. 'Reluctant' – the more lenient term used today, would perhaps be more accurate, for looking back I think much of my 'backwardness' was mainly due to two reasons. There was far too much being 'read to' at an age when I should have been trying to read to myself, while the few books given me to encourage the process were either too juvenile or too advanced for my years. The result was that one rejected the former with contempt after the first page, while the latter, which seemed invariably given over to long descriptive writing before any plot or characters emerged, were equally daunting, involving as they did far more concentration and perseverance than I possessed.

S'wark, in her first few months with us had persuaded my mother to take in the long-standing children's monthly magazine *Little Folks*. I enjoyed being read to from it. There was an exciting serial story, a lot of very good illustrations, and, a great feature, a full colour picture with each number. But as a helpful adjunct in encouraging my reading ability, it had, if anything, rather the reverse effect, for not only were the very banal stories intended for younger readers, all too reminiscent of those in my hated reading books, but they were printed in extra large type and bore the, to me anyway, offensive title 'Pages For Very Little Folk'. In the other magazine, though it too had stories for all ages, I remember nothing so condescending. On the whole I think it was directed more to boys than to girls – certainly the nautical story that was so to possess me had an essentially masculine flavour. It was what might be described as a 'gripping' tale – exciting from the first few paragraphs. It was originally read to me by the younger of my sisters. I then read it, more or less through, by myself – parts of it again and again. It was, I now realise, instructive in an unobtrusive way. Apart from the nautical details, I learnt a great deal of geography from it and an abiding interest in Spain, Portugal and their respective off-shore islands. It was only in adult life I was to discover it was written by H. de Vere Stacpoole, the celebrated author of *The Blue Lagoon*.

Apart from their gripping – and even condescending pages – both these magazines were to introduce a new element into

my immediate future and many, many years later be indirectly responsible for shaping the pattern of my future life.
Both had pages over which someone called 'The Editor'
presided. Readers wrote to him on every conceivable subject
from the right feeding of rabbits to the best way to clean a
bicycle. There were competitions – mostly puzzles – in which
I had never had any interest and, particularly in *Little Folks*
notes about various charitable institutions in which the
Editor invited both interest – and cash. In addition to these
editorial pages there were advertisements, some of them
offering Free Samples.

I was already an ardent applicant for these which I
sometimes saw advertised in a fashion journal patronised by
my mother. Unlike reading, writing had never presented any
difficulties to me and by now mine was not obviously childish
but more or less 'formed', as the expression was. Usually I
wrote my requests in the third person – 'Miss Garnett would
be obliged' etc., having heard my mother consulting S'wark
by reading aloud similar missives to various London shops.
In return for these requests I would receive miniature cakes
of soap or tubes of toothpaste; tiny bottles of scent; little
packets of biscuits or of patent baby-foods. My family were
amused and good-naturedly provided stamps. Then came a
dramatic occurrence. Somewhere – more likely in my
mother's magazine than my own – a firm eulogising their
super wheat-laden bread announced that, should this be
unobtainable at your local baker's, you had only to write to
the Managing Director giving the shop's name and address
and a Sample Loaf – free of all charge – would be yours.

At this period we baked at home so patronised no local
baker. Even so, I was determined to receive the super-
charged wheaten loaf. This time I did not write in the third
person but, as requested in the advertisement, to the Managing Director, beginning 'Dear Sir' and ending 'Yours truly',
followed by my full quota of initials and surname.

A few days later the postman delivered a parcel addressed
'Mrs E. C. R. Garnett'. I was on the look out for him, seized
and opened it to reveal a small, beautifully packed and
highly nutritious-looking loaf which I hid in the toy cup-

board before going off to school, intending to produce it as a 'surprise' at tea-time.

The same afternoon, playing in the garden awaiting the said tea-time, I saw a strange gentleman approach the front door and ring the bell. The parlour-maid evidently regarded him suspiciously for she left him on the mat and went in search of my mother who shortly appeared, to be greeted by the said gentleman, hat in hand and with a low bow and the information that the firm he represented were deeply distressed to learn she was unable to obtain their special bread from her local baker (whose name she had unfortunately omitted to give in her letter) but had only to supply for matters to be immediately remedied.

Somewhat taken aback my mother explained she knew nothing whatever of the matter; had written no letter and actually had no local baker, all bread for the household being made by her cook.

The gentleman had looked puzzled. 'Mrs E. C. R. Garnett?' he enquired – and produced my letter. I was called, my letter handed me and an explanation demanded – and given, the representative his mouth half open regarding me with undisguised astonishment . . .

There was no row. It was agreed I had acted 'in good faith' as a solicitor might say, but it was decreed that in future 'all Free Sample letters must be shown to a grown-up or' (a vital necessity) 'there will be no postage-stamp!'

It was neither Correspondence nor Advertisements but 'The Editor' whoever – or whatever – he was, that really intrigued me and was eventually to take over my rôle as a Naval officer. Soon both he and his 'page' were so to possess me that one night I had a strange dream . . .

As I was to write, over a year later, '*The Poppy* was thought of in a dream' . . . It was; and very soon after the dream became reality, for *The Poppy* was a magazine – and I an Editor!

The first number of *The Poppy* consisted of four pages of unruled paper approximately eight by six inches. This I soon realised was not large enough to include the various contents, and while the unruled paper was an advantage for the 'illustrations', the cover and full page 'frontispiece', ruled paper was more helpful for the Editor's handwriting and what might be called the prose content, though prose in this context included some verse. I compromised; the next and subsequent numbers consisted of four sheets of an exercise book – eight pages in all – with narrow ruled lines, and folded round them, cut to the same size a piece of cartridge paper – known always to me as 'drawing paper', the whole pinned together at the central pages with a couple of ordinary dressmaking pins. The price, which had been a modest half-penny for the first number was raised to a penny. The last page of all gave a list of 'subscribers', their respective addresses and the request not to keep the magazine – as it was grandly called – too long, but to pass it on to the next address on the list as soon as read, the last recipient returning it to the Editor.

Such of the contents as I remember consisted of the said coloured 'Frontispiece'; a serial story, the first of which was entitled 'Cecil: or a True Hero'; a quite atrocious poem – usually something of seasonal or national interest; an editorial page which comprised some notes by the Editor and occasional letters from subscribers; and a page evidently regarded as the high-light of the production for it was headed in large block capitals which announced briefly 'Competions'. All 'Competions' began with the words – soon to become a family slogan – 'All you have to do . . .' followed by details of the said 'Competion'. A prize – sometimes two – was offered. 'Some of my own hair-pins tied up with a bit of pink wool', the elder of my sisters on winning one once caustically but justifiably complained. Both she and my other sister good-naturedly 'took in' the magazine, originally I think out of sheer kindness, the elder adopting the, to me, delightful pseudonym and address, 'Lady Pinkie, Pimpley Park, Portsea-on-the-Plage'; the younger, more modest, keeping her own name but 'The Mousehole, Local' as her address. She also occasionally contributed a short story or other material to fill in space when the Editor, as sometimes happened, ran short of ideas.

By my contemporaries, for whom I originally largely intended the magazine, it was regarded scornfully or with indifference. There was nothing 'exciting' about it; even the 'Competions' failed to attract – one smug child remarking derisively, 'You've spelt it wrong!' I realise now, of course, that it was the general naïveté that attracted and amused adults; for that is what happened. My sisters had read aloud to friends some of the more glaring crudities and sentimentalities; extracts such as that from the current serial, concerning the tragically separated lovers for whom 'there was only the penny post to unite them'; or lines from a poem entitled 'Spring' – with special emphasis on the fury of March winds – which proclaimed:

> 'When at last they stop again
> Everything looks so insane"

and, among other discomforts that:

> 'To go in a motor
> Makes you look like a bloater" . . .

The friends had apparently exploded in gales of, to me, unseemly laughter, but one result was that quite a lot of subscribers were recruited. The Navy was to the fore again and in due course *The Poppy* was being read in more than one gunroom – even as time went on and promotions occurred, a wardroom or two.

Promotion was slow and junior officers in both Services were constantly bewailing the absence of any war – however remote, that would remedy this – something that, even then, once I realised its implications, struck me as singularly macabre.

But they had not long to wait . . . The German Kaiser's constant additions to and boastings about, his fleet were becoming more and more disturbing and those old enough to remember would allude darkly to what was usually referred to briefly as '1870'.

That the Navy was with us again was sudden – and unforeseen. Some friends of my father's living a short distance from us had an only – and obviously adored – son, a Naval Lieutenant. Some time before our arrival his ship had left for a distant part of the Empire. Now – almost literally out of the blue for she had been in tropical waters, she was coming back, and Rickie, as he was called, expected on long leave at any moment. Owing to the eulogies of his adoring parents and an equally adoring aunt who lived with them, I think everyone was slightly apprehensive in regard to this paragon of a son. But the fears proved groundless. He turned out to be a quiet, friendly young man; simple-minded in the best sense of that term – what to myself I always called 'true' – meaning, literally, sincere. He was tall, fair-haired and very thin – a startling contrast to his abnormally obese relatives. I liked him from the start – very largely because he was what I have described as 'true'. But there were other reasons; he did not 'make up' to me as the various suitors had done; there was no cajolery or bribery, and if he laughed at me – as he frequently did – often hilariously, it was somehow kindly laughter, never supercilious or sarcastic, and sometimes, when I got to know him better, accompanied by a hearty slap on the shoulders. There was just one occasion when I felt he had overdone it. This concerned a coloured 'frontispiece' in *The Poppy* of which to my great joy he had become an ardent admirer. The illustration in question with which I was, secretly, rather pleased, depicted what was intended to be a tall and beautiful young lady (in reality a rather gaunt and grim-faced female). She was attired in an orange satin and lace evening dress, high-heeled shoes and adorned with a string of pearls and long dangling earrings, and standing, one hand on hip, sniffing at a bunch of flowers. This masterpiece was entitled 'His Idyll' and I learnt later it had brought down the house – or its equivalent, in more than one gunroom of His Majesty's Fleet. This, combined with Rickie's mirth, I sensed was not complimentary. The reason I did not understand, and was rather hurt. But this incident apart, he was kind and helpful in very many ways. When on leave he frequently did my arithmetic 'prep' for me; could always be relied on to 'stick up' for me, as we called it, in any conflict with authority, and he was not only an admirer of *The Poppy* but recruited several subscribers – and not all from the Navy. I particularly remember one – a Mr R. Bing to whom in spite of insistent family protests I would persist in addressing in any correspondence 'Mr R. Bing, Esq'. His postal address was brief – 'The Stock Exchange, London', but what position he held I never knew. He was a conscientious subscriber paying his subscription and forwarding the copy of the magazine with commendable promptness. He was also an occasional entrant for the 'Competions', once winning a prize, though for what and of what the prize itself consisted, I have forgotten.

*   *   *   *   *

The Poppy continued in existence for two years or so. On the anniversary of its first 'publication' I decided this was worthy of recognition and a notice to this effect duly appeared. 'Today,' it began, 'is Poppy Day' (words in so different a context then mercifully hidden in the future). 'Quantities of Poppies,' it continued, 'are brought to the Editor as he sits at his desk.' It then occurred to me it was May and Poppies do not normally bloom then so after a little thought this was amended to 'forced Poppies'. The Editor's desk, incidentally, was not a desk in the accepted sense but my sisters' old dolls' house, turned back to front, its erstwhile rooms housing the editorial correspondence etc.

Rickie's delight in doing my arithmetic 'prep' equalled mine at getting it done! I had now left The Convent and the amount of 'prep' at the 'mixed' school was overwhelming. Rickie, his long leave over, was now away on some 'Course', mercifully near enough to enable him to come home at weekends, for it was then the amount of 'prep' was apt to be particularly overwhelming. As I have said elsewhere figures, as with most of the family, were practically meaningless. With much misery I had more or less – mostly less – mastered the four 'Rules', i.e. Addition, Subtraction, Multiplication and Division, and very simple money sums. But the new school demanded Fractions and Decimals, and 'Problems' such as two men filling identical baths – one of which leaked so many gallons every five minutes – or something equally absurd and useless. Sometimes Rickie brought a brother officer – a Commander – home with him and he too would come and join in the 'prep', and, very greatly to my delight, the two of them would argue about leaking baths and other similar idiocies.

Unfortunately my form mistress lived in a nearby village, she knew many of my sisters' friends – including the two young men in question. As it was a rarity for me to get any sum right she was never deceived for a moment. 'Is this Lieutenant Shaw's work or Commander Hughes'?' she would enquire blandly when I presented my exercise book on Monday morning . . .

Apart from the interest in *The Poppy* and the 'prep', Rickie's helpfulness extended to conflicts with authority and the memory of one such occasion remains vividly with me. While at The Convent, in what was called 'Le Dessin', I had watched some older girls decorating small wooden boxes and vases and, particularly, narrow strips of wood designed to ornament the space between a mantelpiece and the grate beneath it with what was called 'poker work'. The process fascinated me and I begged Mère St Geniève – as always in charge – to be allowed to try my hand at it, but was told abruptly, '*Non*! C'est pour les grandes filles *seule*ment,' accent on 'seule' and, to make sure there was no misunderstanding, adding in English, 'It is for zee *big* girls *only*'. I was disappointed but soon forgot about it. Some months later and now at the new school, evening 'prep' for once disposed of early, I was sitting idly beside the school-room fire, when the incident suddenly recurred to me. At the same moment I was aware that immediately before me was a narrow, oblong piece of white-painted unblemished wood – simply *asking* to be decorated.

In two minutes I had the brass-topped poker heating in the flames; in less than five it was red hot. In not much more, what was meant to represent a decorative classic frieze – an undulating, squiggly, brown line with blobs here and there representing leaves, adorned what had once been unsullied wood. A scorching smell permeated the room and to my concern some of the 'leaves' still sizzled slightly where the poker had pressed rather too deeply. I stood regarding the finished product with some disappointment, realising sadly its resemblance to what I had intended was very far from perfect, when the door burst open and my father rushed in exclaiming at the smell of burning and demanding, 'What on earth is going on here?' . . . A blazing row was imminent. Fortunately Rickie had not long arrived on some errand. He also had smelt burning and fearing an accident had followed my father upstairs, my mother and sisters hurrying after him.

'Poker-work, by Jove!' he cried, quickly sensing the storm about to break, 'Poker-work! The real thing!' and he picked up the blackened poker which was still emitting little fiery sparks here and there.

'She might have set the whole house on fire!' my father replied furiously. 'And she's ruined the mantelpiece – *ruined* it!'

'Even the shelf above is scorched!' cried my mother.

'But she *meant* awfully well, sir!' said Rickie turning to my father. 'I mean it's an awfully difficult thing to do. A decorative classic frieze; that's what it's meant to be, isn't it?' he turned to me. I nodded, sniffing and tears beginning to roll down my face.

'An awfully difficult thing to do,' repeated Rickie turning to each of my parents in turn. 'Getting the curves in the right places and those – er – leaves and all! Given the proper tools you know she could have made a pretty effective piece of decoration!'

My father had cooled down now. 'It's going to be a pretty effective piece of carpentry for me!' he said, or words to that effect, while my mother kept trying to waft away the fumes with her handkerchief and begging someone to open the window wider.

My sisters glanced at Rickie with undisguised admiration and the elder mutely handed me a handkerchief . . . I forget what actually happened next, only Rickie offering to 'lend a hand' with the 'restoration' . . .

*   *   *   *   *

As time went on it did not escape my attention, now alerted to such matters, that Rickie was becoming attracted to the younger of my sisters. She liked him – as we all did, and enjoyed his company, but she gave him no encouragement and I think now he was probably the kind who needed it. Probably too, she had not entirely 'got over the last affair' as it would have been termed. Given a little more time things might have turned out differently; I would certainly have welcomed him rapturously as a brother-in-law.

But it was not to be. In the late spring of 1916 he was transferred to the cruiser *Hampshire* – the ship later chosen to convey Lord Kitchener on a special mission to Russia. On the afternoon of June 5th soon after leaving port in a violent storm, she struck a German mine a few miles off Marwell Head on the West coast of Orkney and sank almost immediately. There were only twelve survivors.

CHAPTER 7

'This dreadful education business'

First School – Part 1

WITH ONE DAUGHTER leaving school and a second soon to do so – or so she believed at the time, my mother decided a resident governess for me was unnecessary. I too must go to school. 'This dreadful education business' again! A day school first of course . . .

The question was, which school? There were three to choose from. A small and very select establishment some distance from where we lived; a larger one, much nearer, described as 'very mixed' – the mixture referring to social status rather than to gender; nearer still a Convent school. The select establishment was definitely too far away – especially on wet winter mornings; the mixed one considered but rejected. (I was later to go there and made many firm friends among the 'mixed'.) The Convent seemed the obvious choice. But alas, it was not only French it was also Roman Catholic.

My mother, like most Irish Protestants of her day was strongly – almost ferociously – anti-Catholic. Indeed at this period of her life she might fairly be described as extremely bigoted, while the bitter memories of the French way of life experienced in her schooldays still lingered. My father, who had spent three impressionable years at Caen in Normandy, mixing daily with Catholic families and returning to England unscathed and with a great love of France was more tolerant.

K's children, he insisted, naming a friend, attended the school apparently unharmed; there would be excellent opportunities for learning French . . .

I imagine that a great deal of argument and discussion

must have taken place; but time was getting on and eventually my mother was persuaded to make discreet enquiries among her acquaintances concerning attempts at conversion, idolatrous teaching, and other possible perils calculated to ensnare the Protestant child. *Little* children, she was assured, were *safe* . . .

'It is when they grow *older*, you know' . . . while the Rector's wife went so far as to confide to her that if it were not for the uproar it would cause in the parish her own daughters would undoubtedly have been among the pupils. Finally my parents attended some kind of 'Open Day'. My father, engaging in conversation with the nuns and so flattered by their comments on his French – 'sans accent!' – the highest praise, so delighted to hear the French language again, was an easy prey; while my mother, so impressed with examples of the children's sewing and embroidery – she sewed beautifully herself and the art was a 'must' for us from the time we could hold a needle – that my enrolment was almost decided.

An interview between the Reverend Mother, whose English was limited, and my own mother followed soon after. No, she was assured 'zee Protestant children' took *no* part in *any* religious ceremony (which was true); received *no* religious instruction except from 'Zee' Old Testament (which was not). The French language was apparently almost automatically absorbed (never, alas, by me); while three afternoons a week were entirely devoted to 'zee needlework'. The nuns would be delighted to receive 'la petite Ève' at the beginning of the approaching term. The matter was practically settled. But my parents had reckoned without Uncle Herbert.

'The Convent!' he thundered, 'The *Convent*! You must be mad! She will be *turned*! Remember poor Edmund!'

Edmund was the only one of his five brothers who, like himself, had not been installed by their foolishly ambitious mother in an expensive regiment, with totally inadequate means, a situation inevitably leading to disaster.

Edmund, the story went, had been sent at the age of eighteen or so to some friends to convalesce after a bad illness, and been converted to Roman Catholicism by a small boy who passed every Sunday on his way to Mass through woods adjoining the house, singing so sweetly that Edmund, who was very musical, was enchanted. Conversation ensued, books were lent. Conversion followed, and in due course Edmund was ordained. He eventually became a priest at the London Oratory and later its Director of Music, remaining there, a much loved figure, until his relatively early death. My father always spoke of him with affection; of his strong sense of humour and his gusto for the comic songs of the period. His rendering of 'The Road to Mandalay', 'where there aren't no Ten Commandments, an' a man can raise a thirst . . .', was apparently a tour de force, or what today would be described as 'a smash hit'.

Uncle Herbert's sense of humour was, alas, rudimentary. 'You must be mad!' he repeated. 'She will be turned I tell you, turned!'

I happened to be present when this storm broke. 'Turned.' What did it mean? Later, in the calm of her bedroom I questioned one of my sisters. 'It only means they'll try to make you a Roman!' A Roman? My knowledge of Romans was derived entirely from pictures. Helmeted, breast-plated soldiery were scattered throughout my New Testament. The centurion Jairus pleading for his daughter; the Crucifixion squad dicing for Christ's clothing; the sentry guarding St Paul 'in his own hired house'; while in the early pages of my illustrated *History of England* Roman Legionaries were depicted coldly regarding St Gregory among the 'Angeli'; stubbornly defying mobs of Ancient Britons, or confronting the Queen of the Iceni frenziedly driving a chariot into their ranks.

I was horrified! And . . . how was it *done*? More accurate details followed. They need not have worried. I was in no danger of conversion. Probably more of my mother's prejudices had been absorbed than was realised. I was also, among other social activities, on occasional going-to-tea terms with a Roman Catholic family. The long prayers they seemed compelled to learn and their frequent attendances at church I found very daunting. A statue in one of the bedrooms had shocked me profoundly . . . the second Commandment was very obviously being broken . . . while the discovery that both girls and boys wore medals round their necks – even when bathing – though the boys sometimes tried to hide theirs – had not only surprised but in some way I could not have explained, repelled me. But I think the mainspring of my willingness was the joy of scoring off Uncle Herbert. Something of the same sentiment may have occurred to my parents. There are limits to the authority of an uncle however great one's obligations to his kindness and benevolence in the past – and Uncle Herbert had been kind and benevolent in the extreme.

Lacking in humour, perhaps, but a man of extreme rectitude and high moral principles at their Victorian best, he had been despatched with a very small sum of money, immediately after leaving Oxford to try his luck in what were then called 'the Colonies'. He arrived in Australia at a time when the price of land, so his youngest daughter was to tell me in later years, was at its lowest and could be acquired with little more effort than standing beside – better still sitting on – a fence, pointing with a stick at such empty acres as one fancied. Allowing for exaggeration Uncle Herbert certainly managed to purchase large tracts of land for very little money, investing the remainder in sheep to graze them. Australian wool was just beginning to come into its own; before long it was, if one can use the expression in regard to it, booming. As a result of these conditions Uncle Herbert was soon a very wealthy man. But life in Australia did not appeal to him and before long he had sold both land and sheep and returned to England, married and started a family. By now the results of his mother's absurd ambitions were beginning to make themselves felt. Compelled with totally inadequate private means to follow the expensive way of life in their respective regiments, his brothers were perpetually in debt. As the only member of the family with any money, Uncle Herbert was hailed as a heaven-sent benefactor, constantly appealed to for loans, allowances and the payment of bills. My grandfather – always apparently the black sheep of the family, was the worst offender. Married at twenty; wild, reckless, over fond of cards and of alcohol, the

deplorable conditions prevailing in his regiment when sta-
tioned in India at the time of his marriage – conditions to be
publically condemned in later years – were undoubtedly
responsible for a great deal. For a time after returning to
England matters improved but eventually deteriorated,
going from bad to worse. Again and again Uncle Herbert
admonished, made loans, paid debts. His brother was rapidly becoming a misery to his wife and an impossible father.
Finally he was persuaded to resign his commission. Shortly
after, following the barbarous but not uncommon custom of
the time in dealing with refractory relatives, with nothing
but his meagre Captain's pension, he was what was called
'shipped out' to Australia to make his way as best he could
and where five years later, he died.

Meanwhile his children – two boys and a girl – were
'running wild' – especially the boys. The comment of a
porter, overheard at the local railway station, that 'it were
high time they two young gentlemen were sent to a prepa-
ratory school' probably voiced the opinion of many – not
least Uncle Herbert himself. But no prepa-ratory school for
him. Apart from his nephews he had their mother and sister
to consider. At that time boys were received at Public
Schools at a much earlier age than today. Killing two birds
with one stone, Uncle Herbert installed mother and daughter in a small house in the neighbourhood of a well-known
one, and at the tender ages of nine-and-a-half and eleven,
enrolled his nephews there – first as day-boys, later as
boarders.

But to have made money in Australia was one thing; to
invest it successfully in England another. Either Uncle
Herbert had no real business acumen or he was unlucky.
Whatever the reason, before long his investments began to
fail while his capital – already eroded by the constant
demands made on him had dwindled alarmingly. Drastic
retrenchments in his own family were made; all payments to
his brothers curtailed and finally stopped. But the investments continued to decline; very soon Uncle Herbert was no
longer an even moderately wealthy man. Finally a crisis was
reached; every penny was needed for his own, by then,

rapidly increasing, family, and at the vital ages of fourteen and a half and sixteen, my father and his brother, the former already in the top form with a good chance of a classical scholarship to Oxford, were abruptly removed from their school.

My grandmother, a spirited and courageous woman brought up in an austere Scottish home, wasted no time. With her sons and her eleven-year-old daughter she departed for Caen in Normandy, living in France reputed to be cheaper than in England at that time. Even so there was little more than for bare necessities – certainly not enough for the boys to attend the local Lycée for while the schools of most religious orders had recently been abolished, the Ferry Decrees implementing free secular education were not yet law; fortunately they were soon to become so and both boys were later able to attend Courses and Lectures at the University.

In the meantime some haphazard instruction of a curiously miscellaneous nature was provided by a series of indigent ex-teachers. Drawing, including the then fashionable art of china-painting, was among the curricula, 'taught', my father would tell us, 'by a chap who did fakes of Sévres'.

At the end of three years, to avoid compulsory service in the French Army, equipped with a fair knowledge of French history and literature; the decimal system and the art of china-painting, but with an almost perfect command of the French language, the family returned to England. Uncle Herbert's finances had improved slightly but he was in no position to help anyone. His nephews and niece must fend for themselves – and for their mother. Like the relatives of Captain Reece in 'The Bab Ballads', 'It was their duty and they did'.

Now, old but active, Uncle Herbert still liked – and expected – to assert his authority. A stand had to be made. Politely but firmly my father told him the matter of the Convent school was decided. On this occasion I was not present. I only knew that Uncle Herbert had evidently been what I rather horribly called 'squashed'. I was going to The Convent.

No flower-scents can be said to have dominated my first entry into the world of school, only the all-embracing scents of early autumn. Not until the following spring when I became a boarder for a short time did one indeed reign supreme; the heady, almost cloyingly sweet scene of Hawthorn blossom. But the autumnal scents permeated all my first few weeks. Potent and all-pervading columns of thin bluish smoke spiralled upwards from innumerable gardens large and small. Equally – if not more potent, in the grounds of The Convent itself, was a mixture compounded of newly-fallen leaves, grass and earth, scuffed up by the boots of vociferous little boys feverishly searching for 'Conkers'. Little girls scuffed too – myself among them – less vigorously perhaps but no less avidly. The quarry, however, was different; nothing so barbarous as ammunition for Conkers, but the relatively rare, flat-topped chestnuts that with the aid of pins and short lengths of silk or wool could be transformed into dolls' furniture.

It was on one of these autumn-scented mornings that, escorted by my mother, I set forth for my first day at school. In one hand I clutched a dark blue cotton bag with a pair of indoor shoes, and in the other a brown paper parcel containing a garment then indigenous to all French schools, a black overall.

We lived at the top of a long and very steep hill; the main road ran past the foot of it, and on the far side was The Convent. The hazard of crossing this relatively busy highway had caused nearly as much controversy as the risk of conversion. Even in this small country town cars were now outnumbering horses and were apt to come rushing round the corner by the Presbytery – some three hundred yards away – at dizzying speeds of twenty-five to thirty miles an hour. Bulb horns were still in vogue however, and as they were always vociferously sounded at corners one was really in greater danger from the various swiftly trotting horse-drawn vehicles – even from furiously bicycling errand boys. For some time now I had been receiving lessons in what today would be called 'Road Safety' – of the 'Stop, Look,

Listen' variety, but on this, my first day, my mother was with me.

As we neared the bottom of the hill The Convent came into view, its starkly new vermilion roof and glaring white walls rearing up and effectively screening the mellow stone house and big garden behind them. The old house had once been the home of a well known cleric, celebrated alike for his literary achievements and his violently anti-Catholic views. By a nice irony, a teaching Order exiled from France by the Ferry Decrees which drove so many monks and nuns to take refuge in England, was seeking larger premises. The old house with its big rooms and high walled secluded garden came up for sale and was eagerly snapped up. In due course the raw red-roofed school buildings had been built; the cleric's drawing room – a Popish altar at its eastern end, a Holy Water stoup inside the large white-panelled folding doors, became the nun's chapel, while the austere study where some of his more famous books had been written, was used alternately for music practice and the bathing of the younger pupils.

As we reached the end of the hill I could see several children waiting outside the dark red Convent door. Two or three of them I knew slightly from encounters at a weekly dancing class and Christmas or birthday parties.

Before crossing the main road we duly stopped, looked, and listened. My mother consulted her watch; it was exactly five minutes to nine-thirty – the hour of admission for the younger children. Nothing more lethal than a baker's van and a whistling errand boy on a bicycle went by. We crossed safely over and joined the group outside the dark red door – seven or eight boys and girls some of whom were banging impatiently on it. I was suddenly overcome with acute shyness. The children I knew grinned in a rather sheepish way, uncertain, as part of the herd how they should receive me. Those banging on the door turned round, looked briefly and disdainfully at me and resumed their banging while the rest stood stolidly staring in what appeared to me a distinctly hostile silence. After what seemed an agonisingly long time there was a sound of heavy, plodding footsteps. The little barred grille opened with a sharp jerk and a pale, pudding-faced nun, her mouth drooping in a disapproving crescent, her eyes almost hidden behind thick lensed steel-rimmed glasses, peered out from behind the bars. Seeing the assembled company she closed the grille with a bang. There was a rattling of keys and the door opened about half way.

'Bonjour ma Mère! Bonjour ma Mère!' shouted the children jostling each other and trying to push past the stout, dumpy little figure.

'Doucement! Douce*ment*! Peg*gie* – Bet*tie* – Vee*ctor*.' She struggled valiantly but irritably with the English names – then apparently became aware of my mother and myself. To repeated and totally unheeded cries of 'Doucement! Douce-*ment*!' the children rushed past her and disappeared from view down a dark passageway. The nun peered short-sightedly and suspiciously at us. A new pupil? she enquired, ah! she would fetch Reverend Mother, and she beckoned us inside, shut the door and led us to a room at one side of the small dark entrance hall. The Parlour . . . would we please asseyez-nous . . . she would fetch Reverend Mother at once, and she plodded away, shutting the door silently behind her.

The 'Parlour' was a small, rather dark apartment, its highly polished parquet floor smelling of beeswax. In the middle of the room stood a round, equally highly polished table, and exactly in the centre of it, on a circular crocheted mat, a Hound's-tongue fern in a circular green bowl. Flanking the bowl, precisely equidistant from each other, reposed three very ornately bound books each displaying a velvet, gold fringed book-marker. Against one wall hung a small bracket with a statue of the Virgin and Child from which my mother immediately averted her eyes, and on the opposite wall a picture on which I riveted mine. It was a copy of a well known religious engraving and portrayed Christ haloed and clothed as usual, but pointing to His chest where the clothing seemed to have disappeared to reveal a stylised heart – such as those seen on playing cards or old fashioned Valentines, but edged about with flames. I was still lost in contemplation of this, to me, extraordinary representation, when the door opened and the Reverend Mother glided – I use the word advisedly – into the room.

Over crossed hands half hidden under her voluminous sleeves she bowed courteously to my mother and cast a faint smile at me. She had the serene but rather secular face of a late Renaissance Madonna; her English was halting, interspersed with French.

Ah yes, . . . she remembered, she had of course already met my mother and my so-amiable father . . . and this – she turned to me – this was la petite Ève – une petite fille bien élevée she was sure? All of which meant nothing to me except an even stronger than usual aversion to the French language and a fixed determination never to acquire it. The matter of milk at eleven, the exact hour of release and return in the afternoon and my mother, tears in her eyes, prepared to depart. She told me later she wept the whole way home up the steep hill and was distinctly mortified on returning to fetch me at twelve-thirty to learn that I had not shed a single tear!

Meanwhile, clutching my shoe-bag in one hand and the parcel with my black pinafore in the other, I followed the Reverend Mother down a short stone passage to a large glass-roofed, stone-floored playground. A broad white line divided it in half, red painted wooden benches surrounded it on three sides, while on the fourth stood a cupboard with a half-drawn brown curtain revealing rows of pigeon holes filled with an assortment of boots and shoes. Immediately facing one as one entered were half-glazed double swing-doors, intersecting the red benches and leading directly to the main school, while in the extreme right-hand corner a small door led to what I was later to learn were the nuns' private quarters. Now, like so many of her kind, a nun seemed to emerge silently from nowhere. The Reverend Mother spoke some words to her, bowed to my mother, nodded kindly to me, and, equally silently, glided away and disappeared through the small door in the corner. The nun smiled gravely at me then, opening one half of the swing doors went into the corridor beyond, opened a nearby door there and putting her head round it murmured something in

French. From within came the high-pitched buzz of children's voices and a moment later a child – actually of my own age but several sizes larger – appeared. She wore a black pinafore and round her waist what looked like a dressing-gown cord. It was bright emerald green and ended in two large tassels. Her immensely thick, dark red hair was parted in the middle and hung down her back in two rope-like plaits.

'This,' said the nun, introducing her, 'is Eugénie. She will show you where to put your shoes and hang up your coat and hat, and take you to your class-room.' And smiling at me she went away as suddenly and silently as she had come and disappeared like the Reverend Mother through the small corner door.

Eugénie and I stood glaring at each other like two dogs about to fight. We had needed no introduction for we were old and sworn enemies, for, except in summer, we met weekly at the local dancing-class which Eugénie and another, much older, boarder from The Convent attended. Everyone – grown-ups included – thought Eugénie was French. Her name; her un-English looking silk check dresses; the fact that she was a boarder at a French Roman Catholic Convent, probably helped to foster the illusion. Actually she was more English than myself with my three-parts Celtic ancestry. Her surname was uncompromisingly Anglo-Saxon, and with two or three other Convent boarders she could be seen at Morning Service at the Parish Church every Sunday. Our violent antipathy which had been mutual – and instantaneous (it was later to develop into as fervent a friendship) – was never expressed in words, only by a look of intense loathing, and physically by a violent – often extremely painful – squeezing of hands whenever the opportunity occurred; marching in twos; in 'the Grand Chain' of 'The Lancers'; in various Scottish Reels and other communal dances.

'You put your outdoor shoes *there*,' she announced without further ceremony and pointing to the brown-curtained pigeon-holes, 'and your indoor ones *on*. Your number's 23,' she added and waited whistling under her breath, while I hunted for 23, found it, and did as she had said. Whether the whistling was an assertion of authority or disguise for nervousness I had no means of knowing. I took it for superiority, and it did nothing to lessen my antipathy. As soon as I was ready she stopped whistling, said briefly, 'Come on', and led the way through the swing doors. A long, very wide grey marble floored corridor stretched ahead. On both sides of it were doors, and from behind some came a low buzz of children's voices or the authoritative tone of a nun.

'In here,' said my companion opening a door labelled 'Cloakroom'. She then instructed me to hang up my coat and hat – 'Peg 23' – and put on my pinafore, adding bluntly, 'I suppose you've *got* one?'

'*Of course,*' I replied in as scornful a tone as I could muster and struggled into it, thankful it had no fastenings, but was made with a low cut square neck that went easily over one's head; I was still not very adept at doing up buttons at the back of any garment.

'Here's your Cordelière', she went on after rummaging about in a drawer. 'My *what*?' 'Cordelière. You tie it round you to show what class you're in,' and she handed me a replica of her emerald green dressing-gown cord.

'But I don't *know* what class I'm in,' I objected.

'The bottom one of course,' she said scornfully and walked off into the corridor.

I wrestled successfully with the cord then joined her. She led the way to a door marked 'Class 3', then seizing my hand in one of hers and squeezing it so that tears started in my eyes, with her other she opened the door and pulling me after her, announced loudly, 'Eve Garnett!', dropped my hand like a hot brick, shut the door and went to sit at a desk at the back of the room.

Rubbing my squeezed hand I found myself facing some fifteen boys and girls, gratified to find that if this was the bottom class at least Eugénie was in it too!

*   *   *   *   *

Perhaps because I had never been to any school before, the rules and customs at The Convent appeared less strange than they might otherwise have done; for strange indeed many of them were. Though slightly adapted to English ways and the twentieth century they mostly remained faithful to the original school founded circa 1860 at the Mother house in central France. The 'Bonjour ma Mère', and the kissing on both cheeks of the nun in charge of one's classroom on entering it in the morning; the black pinafores – admittedly indigenous to practically all French schools; the Cordelières already mentioned; the Primes . . .

Primes were slips of paper with a printed design and lettering and one's name written in and were a kind of commentary on one's work and conduct during the preceding week. They were coloured in order of excellence, pink, yellow, blue and white, and handed out at an assembly of the whole school on Monday mornings. I think I only once achieved a pink, very occasionally a yellow, almost always a blue – once or twice a white. A White Prime was the disgrace of disgraces. Once a child in my class received three whites in three successive weeks. What she had done – or not done – I forget, but the denunciation of the Reverend Mother's Second in Command – the fiery, red-faced and always terrifying, Mère St Madeleine who taught the Upper School – and dominated most teaching activities – made one's blood run cold. I remember the victim turning as white as the Prime in her hand though what appalling penance – other than villification before the whole school – she received, I do not know. One was never punished; one 'did A Penance'. This could take many forms whereas 'A Recompence', awarded for good conduct, hardly, if ever, varied, and was what was known as 'A Holy Picture'. These were usually French, occasionally English, but both species were much the same. They were quite small – about four by three inches and were printed on a parchment-like paper, sometimes with serrated gilt edges, and depicted lavishly gold-haloed Saints or Biblical characters with sugary sweet countenances and even more sugary sweet pink and blue garments.

One of the nuns – Mère St Geneviève – who presided over a large studio-like appartment called 'Le Dessin' – and who was always known among us as 'the man of The Convent' owing to her enormous feet and her prowess with a hammer and nails, opening refractory windows and other activities requiring brute-strength, would produce similar, if rather less sugary, creations. It is true she substituted flowers for figures so perhaps the cloying colours were less conspicuous. Beautifully drawn, and inscribed in copper-plate writing these productions were handed out on various special occasions. I myself received one on leaving. An inscription, surrounded by pink roses and intertwining blue ribbons, read, 'To dear Eve from her friends at The Convent' and was followed by a list of names; that several were very definitely not my friends nor I theirs was immaterial.

Feasts and Fasts abounded – the Feasts seeming to outnumber the Fasts. Some of the more important were celebrated by a half holiday and, for the boarders, special food.

Occasionally, like some of the day girls I stayed to tea and was not long in discovering it was best never to do this on a Friday; always if possible on a Thursday, for Thursday was a recognised Feast Day. This meant cake as well as bread and jam on the long narrow refectory tables, whereas on Friday, a very strictly kept Fast Day, bread and butter only would appear.

Certain special occasions – such as the Reverend Mother's Feast for example – entailed mild celebrations. The statues of the Virgin and Child – coloured sculptured editions of the 'Holy Pictures' – that stood on gilded brackets on the walls of every class-room, were half-smothered in flowers – likewise the Reverend Mother herself.

Recitations and musical performances were the order of the day. Every child had to take part. I remember myself, shaking with nervousness, thumping out, with many wrong notes 'A Highland Lad my Love was Born', a then popular 'piece' from a rather terrible compendium used by some music teachers and called an 'Instruction Book'. Even very small children who had just 'begun' music, their legs dangling from the piano stool, solemnly played a scale to much clapping and applause, and smiles and bows from the Reverend Mother.

But from some of the major Feasts – Corpus Christi for

example – Protestants were barred. One was sent home early reluctantly leaving one's Catholic friends, dressed in their best clothes, processing round the grounds with roses in their hands and later, we enviously understood, candles.

In the class-room, of course, one was used to not taking part in what Uncle Herbert – himself what was then known as 'High Church' or, by my mother 'half-way to Rome' – would, undoubtedly, have designated 'Popish practices'. These referred chiefly to the bringing of flowers for the statues already referred to, and participation in the Angelus. Every morning on the stroke of twelve the Angelus bell would begin to ring. All the Catholic children immediately slid to their knees while their Protestant companions sat smugly at their desks staring straight ahead, resolutely resolved to have no part in the recitation of the 'Hail Mary' and the signs of the cross that accompanied it.

Perhaps one of the strangest customs related to baths. At any time after nine-thirty in the morning, whatever lesson was in progress, there might be a gentle tap at the class-room door followed by the appearance of a nun who would nod to the one in charge and holding up a beckoning finger announce softly 'Mary O'Brien's bath', or whatever the name of the candidate. And immediately Mary O'Brien would rise from her desk and like St Matthew, leaving all, follow the beckoning figure from the room. The sequel – a most strange ritual undoubtedly inherited direct and un-changed since 1860 – I was not to discover until I became a boarder for a short period, an experience to be told later.

Another ritual, differing only from its equivalent in schools of today by its setting, or background – and, of course, the quality of the milk – was what might be called the Morning Milk Rite. Precisely on the stroke of eleven o'clock a bell would ring and all the children in the two lowest classes would gather in the cloak-room where glasses of milk on a big black iron tray were carried in by a little Lay Sister. She was pretty and pink-faced and always smiling. Unlike the 'teaching nuns' as we called them, her skirt was short and she wore white stockings. She carried the tray of milk – which must have been very heavy – with an air of gaiety lowering it tenderly on to a table beside the presiding nun. She might have been bringing us champagne!

Alas, the milk was always full of 'skin' and frequently anything but fresh. To drink it normally was nauseating but I soon discovered a technique had been evolved. It was possible, provided one took a very deep breath – and could hold it long enough – to gulp down the milk without tasting it at all. It required practice but I soon became an adept.

Immediately the 'rite' was over it was time for the morning 'break' and we all rushed for the stone-floored play-room where we would jump jerkily up and down for several minutes. This activity was known as 'making cheese'.

I vaguely remember reporting the condition of the milk at home and being told 'nonsense' or not to be 'fussy'. Other children I am sure must have done the same and I am also sure that in our respective homes we would all have refused to drink it. Was it the stern eye of the nun in charge, her calm unquestioning expectation of our obedience? Our herd-like attitude? Whatever the reason I cannot remember anyone ever refusing, however revolting, to drink the milk.

*   *   *   *   *

The teaching was very definitely on the lines of that followed by the Mother House in 1860, or even earlier – the greater part of it by rote. Geography for instance: each child in turn stood in front of a large map of the British Isles armed with a long flexible cane and pointed, as the case might be, at the principal bays, harbours and rivers of England and Wales (Scotland and Ireland for some reason were not included). As one pointed the class recited the names in unison. The rivers always went with a swing, gabbled as quickly as possible with hardly a pause for breath. 'Tyne, Wear, Tees, Ouse, Trent; Witham, Welland, Nene, Great Ouse, Yare, Orwell, Stour, Coln, Chelmer; Thames, Medway'. . . . The bays and harbours rather slower, each name heavily stressed. 'The *Humber*, the *Wash*, The-*Mouth-Of-The-Thames*; *Portsmouth* Harbour, *Southampton* Water; *Poole* Bay, *Tor* Bay, *Plymouth* Sound . . .

The forty English counties, each with its principle towns,

went best of all. There was a sort of satisfaction about the long names and their recitation developed into a kind of chant. 'Northumberland, *Newcastle*, Berwick and *Alnwick*; Durham, *Durham*, Sunderland and *Stockton*; Yorkshire, *York*, Leeds, Sheffield and *Hull*' . . . We went down the east coast and along the south, voices rising higher and higher, and even the least intelligent and most bored child perked up when 'Devonshire, *Exeter*, Plymouth and *Devon*port' was reached. For some reason – could it have been a matter of pronunciation? – the Welsh counties, unlike the Welsh harbours and rivers, were not included. We leapt blithely from 'Gloucestershire, *Gloucester*, Bristol and *Cheltenham* to the counties bordering the north-west coast, and thence to the Midlands. When Worcestershire was reached I always experienced a sense of elation. I felt it was a distinction to have lived in two counties.

Even apart from the Welsh counties there remained hazards of pronunciation. I earned much ridicule from my sisters and raised eyebrows from my parents when, asked at lunch what I had learnt that morning, I replied happily that we had 'done' the Southern counties of England, and proceeded proudly to chant 'Kent, *Canterbury*, Maidstone and *Dover*; Sussex, *Chee-chester*, Brighton, and *Loos*'.

'Mother St Bernard calls them that!' I protested hotly when stopped at this point and corrected. There was a short silence . . . A delicate situation had developed; how correct the child and at the same time uphold the teacher? A blessed compromise was reached. 'Well, you see, Mother St Bernard is *Irish*', and, hurriedly putting the onus on the child, 'Surely you remember going to Lewes when you stayed with Uncle Frank at Framfield?' Henceforth it was Chichester and Lewes at home but Chee-chester and Loos at school. Loyalty to Mother St Bernard? The herd instinct again?

When we had 'done' England we began on Europe. First the capes and harbours. 'North Cape and Nordkyn in *Norway*; the Skaw in *Denmark* . . .' Next the rivers. The Seine, the Rhone, the Rhine; the Danube; the Vistula and Volga; the Don – that still flowed quietly . . .

After the rivers the capitals; Russia – the Revolution was

just round the corner – was still 'St Petersburg-on-the-Neva'. Brief descriptions of each country were given. One paused for a moment at St Petersburg to glimpse the frozen Neva; icicles hanging from houses; desolate plains of snow; droshkys; wolves – the wolves, anyway for me, always pursuing the droshkys . . .

There were hazards of pronunciation affecting Spain – especially the rivers Guadiana and Guadalquivir, but they went unchallenged. My family, mercifully, knew no Spanish. Madrid, 'very hot and dusty', enlivened by bull fights, girls dancing with clapping castanettes, and 'a gallery of very beautiful pictures', remained happily undisturbed 'on the Manzanaries'. 'Germany-Berlin-on-the-Spree' always, of course, brought down the house; Germany – so soon to overshadow and to stain the remainder of one's childhood . . .

The Multiplication Tables were taught on the same lines. These were definitely chanted. 'Six *ones* are six; six twos are *twelve*' . . . Even today, whenever I think of them, I can recall the triumphant ending of any particular table; the rising crescendo when twelve times anything – we never went beyond twelve times – was reached; the mounting excitement when numbers began to go into the hundreds. 'Twelve sevens are eighty-four, twelve nines are *a hundred and eight*!' And the culmination of joy when the grand finale, '*twelve twelves are a hundred-and-forty-four!*' was achieved.

There can be few educationalists today who would countenance such methods. And yet, I wonder . . . Though my mathematical powers are best represented by the letter 'o'; though my maximum marks in any arithmetic examination never exceeded 5%; though Algebra and Geometry have remained, in every sense, a closed book, and all my monetary affairs are conducted in 'ones', where the Multiplication Tables are concerned I am never at a loss, while the nature and whereabouts of Europe's capital cities; the harbours, rivers, and the Counties of England with their chief towns – Chee-chester and Loos notwithstanding – remain fixed for ever in my memory. Small attainments it is true. But can a method that produces such results be wholly valueless?

On the occasions when Father Middleton, the Parish Priest, came to instruct the Roman Catholic children in their Catechism, the Protestants sat at their desks drawing maps. My favourite was the map of Palestine. This was not due to any religious zeal but because it was the easiest – and quickest – to draw. One long slanting line ending in a small jutting pyramid shape, followed by a rather longer slanting line, sufficed for the coast. Inland, near the pyramid shape, a small rectangle represented the Sea of Galilee; a kind of squiggle – the river Jordan – joining it to the larger rectangle of the Dead Sea. Jerusalem, Bethlehem, and Nazareth were duly printed in capital letters, roughly in their respective places – and the job was done! One could then sit back and listen to the questions and answers wafting around one, thankful that the Church of England equivalent – endless as it seemed, – was as nothing to this. Sometimes Father Middleton would glance at one's map. 'Very good,' he would murmur and pat one on the shoulder so that one wondered vaguely if this was an attempt at conversion.

Father Middleton was a charming man, somewhere in his early forties. Tall, thin, with a very white face – he was to die some four or five years later of Pernicious Anaemia which my father, once invited to supper at the Presbytery where the meal had consisted of two very thin slices of ham – one each – and a minute piece of bread and cheese, always maintained was due to starvation. Father Middleton got on well with almost everyone; even Uncle Herbert might have conceded he was a good fellow – if misguided. Among his many activities – he was the only Catholic priest in the area – he had inaugurated a series of what were called 'Lantern Lectures'. Tickets for these, in aid of some charity, were available to the public and the Lectures were given in The Convent. Two of the class-rooms, the wooden partitions between them rolled back, formed the auditorium. Chairs from the Refectory and Chapel were brought in for the adult audience, the Convent boarders and any day boys and girls who attended being accommodated on some narrow benches forming the front row with a watchful eyed nun at the end of each bench to keep order.

Father Middleton had travelled widely in his youth. The cine-camera had not yet made its appearance but he himself with his incredibly prolific series of photographs made into Lantern slides was almost as good as one while his graphic and loving descriptions were equal to – if not better – than many a modern tape recording.

My parents decided to attend the Lectures and to my great joy I was allowed to go too. The fact that they did not begin until eight o'clock – long past my normal bed-time – was an excitement in itself, only eclipsed by the setting out in the dark or sometimes moonlight, or, on frosty nights under the magic of a brilliantly star-lit sky.

It was now that 'The Skinnus' – my earliest but one remembered toy – came into his own again. I already knew slightly a little girl, Peggy, a year or so younger than myself who lived very near us. The child of allegedly Protestant but actually agnostic parents, she had been at The Convent for quite a long time. Now, both in the School and walking back and forth twice a day up the long steep hill to our respective homes, our friendship deepened. We were constantly in and out of each other's houses or conversing on the telephone. These conversations – mainly about our respective play-things or games sometimes lasted so long that the operator would cut us off.

Peggy was the owner of a dolls' house of a sort – I then had only the remains of my sister's old one; she also had a small brother who possessed two 'clock-work' motor cars. These I found fascinating especially when he could be prevailed on to lend them – which was not often – and they could be filled with the inhabitants of his sister's dolls' house and career madly about the nursery floor.

Of my possessions it was 'The Skinnus' that most attracted Peggy. She insisted on taking him out on the road, or rather pavement; sitting astride him and gleefully ex-claiming at the speed he covered the distance between our houses. Why not, she suggested, take it in turns to ride him to school? I demurred. I think I felt too old to be seen riding a toy horse. There was also, I pointed out, the matter of 'The Skinnus'' iron wheels which from long wear and tear were given to becoming wedged in his wooden stand. It took time to dislodge them and would make us late – the unforgivable sin. Peggy reluctantly agreed but after some thought suggested we might go to the Lectures on him. Grown-ups were with us and could help with the wheels and as we were always far too early any delay would not matter. After some consideration and the thrill of a trial run down the hill, I agreed, abandoning the thought I was too old and that anyway it would be dark and no one to see me.

My parents at first refused to agree to the venture but were finally persuaded. 'The Skinnus', his wheels oiled and generally attended to by my father, seemed to warm to his job. We rode him in turns glorying in his, for those days, almost dizzy speed on the steeper parts of the hill and his presence definitely added excitement to an already exciting evening.

The excitement was further increased by the sight of the transformed class-room. At one end on a raised platform, was the magic-lantern apparatus, the vigorous Mère St Geneviève in command of the boxes and boxes of slides, while Father Middleton stood to one side of a big white screen on which they would appear, ready to point at specific items with what looked suspiciously like a fishing rod.

Of the various Lectures I attended, four remain vividly in my memory. Two were almost in the nature of conducted tours. One of Rome, ancient and modern; the other the area of Turkey round Istanbul – or Constantinople as it was then called. St Sophia from every possible angle; the Bosphorus and glimpses of the coast of the always sinister-sounding Black Sea; the then placid Sea of Marmara with the Gallipoli Peninsula and the Dardanelles – names so soon to be tragically and unforgettably projected into one's daily life. The other two lectures, originally given elsewhere, were about the Passion Play at Oberammergau and a relatively recent eruption of Vesuvius at both of which Father Middleton had been present. I think the Passion Play involved more than one lecture and I remember that both the copious photographs and the graphic but quietly spoken commentary impressed me enormously. I think the adult audience was impressed too; I vaguely remember my father and a friend agreeing 'it was as good as being there – and far more comfortable'. But for the juvenile audience it was the pictorially dramatic spectacle and Father Middleton's equally dramatic description of Vesuvius – Vesuvius in full eruption – that delighted – and awed us. The enormous seven to eight mile high cauliflower-like cloud poised above the crater; the volcanic ash and debris shooting hundreds of feet into the sky; the terrifying, almost continuous lightning; the streams of boiling, bubbling, lava; the villagers and animals flying for their lives . . .

The Lectures were an education in themselves. Rome and Naples especially rousing an abiding interest in Italy, her people, her history, her art. But the Lectures also had their lighter side. For most of them – especially the 'tours' of Rome and Turkey – sketch maps were necessary. Father Middleton was poor and he wasted no money on special paper for these, happily drawing them on sheets of lavatory paper. This was clearly recognisable by the rather large perforation marks dividing the sheets of the type of paper then in use and which appeared only too clearly in the lantern slides.

The adult audience may have smiled but the juvenile one on the front benches – especially the younger section, was transformed into a heaving row of suppressed giggles every time a map appeared, while the nuns in charge realising they were unable to control the situation, stared stolidly ahead.

The maps were also responsible for a 'dare' – an experience every school-child knows. Father Middleton, standing to one side of the white sheet on which the slides were shown, his fishing-rod pointer in one hand, in the other held a small tin-like object which, when pressed, made a kind of clicking noise. This was to indicate to Mère St Geneviève to produce the next slide from the carefully numbered collection beside her.

It so happened that one of the younger children had found a similar object in a cracker at some Christmas or birthday party. This was duly displayed and 'clicked' during 'Recreation' as the period after the morning milk-drinking was officially called, and the matter of a 'dare' was immediately conceived. The idea was for someone to use the clicking object during a Lecture, and so cause Mère St Geneviève to produce a slide before the Lecturer was actually ready for it. The inconceivable consequences should anyone achieve this were in no way lessened by the thrilling possibility that someone might – just *might* have the courage to do it . . .

There was a great deal of boasting before the next lecture. 'You just wait and see!' . . . 'What do you bet I won't?' . . . This usually from one of the boys, and much flourishing about by whoever had hold of the object in question. But nothing ever happened. Probably fear of the unknown consequences was too great; perhaps we were too young, not rash enough to take the risk . . . Whatever the reason, Father Middleton's clicking and Mère St Geneviève's correct change of slides continued as before, serenely, uninterrupted.

The evenings ended gloriously. Out into the dark or moon-light or star-light; the climb home up the steep hill, taking it in turn to push 'The Skinnus'. No bath; only 'a quick wash'; Puff in her basket wagging a sleepy but welcoming tail. Then biscuits and milk in bed; good-night kisses; admonishings to 'go to sleep quickly – it's after ten o'clock!' The wonder of this, and, very soon, the eternal wonder, sleep.

First School – Part 3

But perhaps it was only as a boarder that one felt the combined alien and out-dated atmosphere most strongly. 'French', I would be told, briefly and bluntly, if I reported any particularly outstanding peculiarities when I returned home from one of the weekly or fortnightly stays I sometimes experienced if my parents had to be away from home. And French they probably were but French of the mid-nineteenth century rather than the early twentieth as contemporaries being educated at other Convent schools at that time have since confirmed. For example the matter of the strange hours for baths already partly recorded. You left your classroom, followed the beckoning nun to the corridor outside and were immediately despatched upstairs to fetch your sponge, soap and bath-towel. These were kept on a shelf over a row of a dozen or so white porcelain basins more reminiscent of a Victorian boys' preparatory school than an establishment for young ladies. Here, in a long narrow room, morning and evening ablutions took place; in the morning, one and all stripped to the waist, in stone-cold water, completed with an icy dowsing from the nun in charge; in the evening, all of us still fully clothed, an almost ceremonial washing of hands and faces in water said to be hot but usually tepid, before being lined up to march to the adjoining dormitory to undress.

Having collected my belongings I followed the nun down the wide marble-floored corridor. Near the big Play Room doors and exactly opposite the cloakroom, a long narrow passage with windows on one side looking on to the garden, connected the new school buildings with the old original house. The passage ended in a small kind of hall. On the left were the big white and gold double doors of the Chapel, once the drawing room of the previous owner – the literary cleric already mentioned; on the right a similar but smaller door leading into the room which had served as his study. It was not a big room, and except for the now almost empty bookshelves that had once housed his library, the furnishings consisted of an upright piano used for music practice; a piano stool, and three straight backed, uncomfortable wooden chairs. In the middle of the room, looking surprisingly out of place on the highly polished parquet floor, was a blue and white striped bath-mat; and on it, looking even more surprising, a shallow oval-shaped enamel bath; brown without, white within. This was flanked by two huge brown enamel hot water cans – one gently steaming. Over the back of one of the wooden chairs hung a garment, later to reveal itself as a species of paddling drawers of a kind sometimes seen in Victorian pictures of children playing by the sea.

The nun in charge of the proceedings was elderly, her English limited and halting. I felt shy at being expected to undress in the presence of a stranger and was taking my time about it, when I became aware water from the steaming can was being poured into the bath. A moment or so later, to my horror, I was being handed the paddling drawers and in a voluble mixture of French and English, accompanied by a series of pantomime gestures being commanded to put them on, take off my vest, and get into the water to be bathed. I was outraged; I had been bathing myself for some time now though frequently some adult, aware the result was by no means faultless, would take over. I disclosed the former part of this information to the nun and balefully regarding the paddling drawers returned them to her. This let loose a perfect torrent of French and broken English, a handing back of the said paddling drawers and an explanation to the effect that it was not 'comme il faut' – a phrase I was familiar with as often used at home – to be seen, even if alone, at the advanced age of eight 'toute nue'. Overcome, I gave in. As soon as I had arrayed myself in the garment which was the colour of old string – and felt like it – rough and scratchy, the nun pulled my vest over my head, pinned my long, straggly hair into a knot, and smilingly stroking my head repeated her remarks as to what was – or rather was not – 'comme il faut'.

The ceremony over, myself dried and dressed, we returned down the long passage, I to my classroom, she with my washing paraphernalia to the wash-room upstairs.

The lesson I had left was over, another in progress. At playtime I questioned some of my friends who, though no older, were apparently allowed to bath themselves. As for the paddling drawers, no one, I was told, ever thought, even *dreamed* of putting them on! You just 'swished' them about in the bath after you had finished, wrung them out and left them on the bath-mat. Instructions faithfully followed when I eventually managed to convince authority that *at home I bathed myself*.

But there were other curious and out-dated customs. Even the uniform – worn only by the boarders – was a variant of the popular British sailor-suit but of several decades earlier. It consisted of a black serge skirt well below the knee – even for five-year-olds; a blouse to match with a black sateen sailor-collar bordered with three rows of what were originally white machine stitching, but like the V-shaped flannel vest in front had turned a kind of dirty buff colour from frequent washings. With the regulation black pinafore, relieved only by a brightly coloured Cordelière, the result was a distinctly funereal appearance. When I first saw it I was suddenly more aware of – and thankful for – my own apparel; a skirt of the colour then known in shops as 'Light Navy' – a good two-and-a-half inches above the knee – and a jumper to match with either red or green collar and cuffs.

* * * * *

Like all the Protestant children I never took part in the Angelus or other 'Popish Practices' as Uncle Herbert would undoubtedly have called them. My only lapse was on the occasion I first stayed to tea. Before we began Grace was said – standing – and seeing all my companions making the Sign of the Cross, I attempted to follow suit. Apparently my gestures were all in the wrong order and before we sat down I was sternly rebuked and admonished to refrain in future from any such attempts. I had certainly never attended any Chapel service.

As a boarder things were different. Attendance at early morning Chapel was definitely a 'must' for everyone. Possibly it helped to make sure we were all – Catholics and Protestants alike – awake, washed and dressed, at the same time. But I am sure I can never, instinctively perhaps, have revealed to my mother that, my head covered in a kind of white handkerchief, and except for ignoring the Holy Water stoup or making the Sign of the Cross, I daily took part in a short but entirely Catholic service. Had I done so I am sure instant removal from the school would have followed.

Even before I embarked on my first stay as a boarder the Reverend Mother had been approached with searching enquiries concerning the matter of Protestant prayers. The Reverend Mother's command of English – both spoken and understood – was far from perfect but she had assured my mother that 'zee Lord's Prayer and zee private devotions' took place before breakfast each morning, and that 'every evening before zee bed-time' a nun would listen to 'zee Protestant childrens' prayers'. That the Lord's Prayer and 'private devotions' – the latter in my case a brief petition for family and friends and a fervent request for assistance in 'being good' – took place at the Chapel service she conscious-ly – or unconsciously – did not reveal.

One of the great attractions of being a boarder – anyway for myself – was the lateness of bedtime. At home this was still six o'clock though it was usually nearer seven or later before good-nights were said and the gas lamp over the bed 'turned down'. At the Convent eight o'clock was the hour appointed for the younger children but for the Protestants, thanks to the ceremony concerning their prayers it was nearer nine before one was actually in one's bed.

As the Reverend Mother had promised, a nun ready and waiting to hear the Protestant prayers, was at hand. She sat bolt upright on a hard wooden chair while some eight or nine children ranging in age from five to seventeen knelt in a semi-circle before her. Gathering her robes about her as if to avoid contamination, she would clasp her hands together, cast down her eyes and exhort us to 'Commence'.

To my surprise, after the Lord's Prayer the Creed was recited – and I alone of the younger children appeared to know it. This was not virtue on my part. From two-and-a-half to six years old I had lived within a short walk of a Cathedral and from the age of four or five attended its short Sunday morning service.

In the Cathedral we sat on the right of the Nave near the choir-stalls and, like them, sideways to the Altar and as the reciting of the Creed necessitated facing it, a right-about-turn was required. This may well have helped to impress the words on my mind. Later, of course, they were learnt by heart as part of the Catechism. The Doxology ended the ceremony. The nun then rose stiffly from her hard chair, shook out her robes and murmuring 'Bon soir mes enfants' to an answering chorus of 'Bon soir ma Mère' left us. The older girls dispersed to their recreation room, the younger contingent to its dormitory.

The dormitory resembled, as nearly as possible, a hospital ward. Down either side of the long room with its highly polished parquet floor, stood immaculate white painted beds, on each an equally immaculate French 'duvet'. In the centre of the room was a small table such as a Ward Sister might use and on it a tiny, heavily-shaded oil lamp. At one end of the room was a large, white-curtained window overlooking the glass roof of the play-room; at the other something certainly never seen in a hospital ward and to the children the pièce-de-resistance. This was the bed of the nun in charge. And no ordinary bed but a long, narrow four-poster surrounded by white curtains, those at the front looped back like window ones, until such time as its occupant should retire for the night – an event it was the ambition, never to be realised, of every child in the dormitory to witness – likewise that of her morning up-rising.

Once in our respective beds, the electric light switched off, she would seat herself at the little table holding some holy book close to the shrouded lamp, or walk silently up and down softly murmuring prayers or extracts from a religious work. It must have had an hypnotic effect for in a matter of minutes we were all asleep, and remained so until, dressed and smiling, the slowly pacing nun of the night before was walking briskly up and down vigorously ringing a large brass hand-bell and exhorting us: 'Levez-vous vite! . . . Immédiatement!'

*   *   *   *   *

This peaceful, undisturbed sleep was new to me for at home I suffered from extremely alarming nightmares. Ironically it was the teaching of needlework – something in the nature of a casting vote in my mother's decision I should attend the school – that was, directly or indirectly, the main cause of these upheavals. For upheavals they undoubtedly were! Every two weeks or so somewhere between two and three a.m. I would wake, stiff with fright, gripped by some nameless but monstrous terror. After an agonising wait to gather together the little courage I possessed, I would stand up in my bed and turn up the faintly glowing gas above it. Still terrified, but encouraged by the light, I would then rouse the sleeping Puff from her basket behind a curtained-off alcove and clutching her collar drag her across the room, out through the always partly-left-open door, through the hooked-back one of the corridor beyond, finally arriving shivering with cold, fright – or both – at my parents' or the bedroom of a sister, complaining vaguely of 'bad dreams.'

It was most often my eldest sister's room. It was the nearest and she, relatively, the most welcoming occupant. My other sister was a heavy sleeper and reluctant awakener – seldom welcoming; her room was also the furthest off. Should the pilgrimage end in my parents' room which was between the other two, my long-suffering father would settle the matter quickly by getting up and going off to spend the rest of the night in my bed, thereby causing mingled surprise and alarm to the house-maid when, in due course, she arrived with the morning hot-water can. Meanwhile, Puff, her mission accomplished, would have returned to her warm basket.

Both my sisters' beds were small, narrow ones and they would complain bitterly of my cold feet as I snuggled in beside them – and even more bitterly when a few minutes later the drama would end with my announcing, 'I've left the light on', and they would feel constrained to get up and go and put it out.

One cause of these nightmares was, as I have written, the needlework class. These sessions, conducted by Mother St Bernard, took place three afternoons a week from two until four. One began one's instruction with what was grandly called 'Tapestry' – in my case a cushion top composed of squares, oblongs and other geometric-like shapes filled in with lengths of brightly coloured wool. From Tapestry one advanced to 'Broderie Anglaise' and at the end of my first year, bursting with pride of achievement I took home a by-no-means well embroidered white collar of the kind then worn as an adornment to a winter or summer dress. I was allowed to wear it and would smugly enjoy comments on my prowess and the evident efficiency of The Convent teaching commented on by assorted visiting adults.

'Plain sewing', as it was called, was last on the list, the idea being to encourage what, for most, was their first handling of a needle, with something more stimulating than hemming or the making of button-holes. Even so, for most of us 'needlework afternoons' were long and laborious and by way of stimulation Mother St Bernard would enliven the time with, of all things, ghost stories!

She had an apparently inexhaustible selection – each seemingly more exciting, thrilling – and horrifying – than the last. I, as I think most of the children did, adored them – but only at the time of their telling. Then they were stories, thrilling, absorbing; at other times – walking alone in slowly-gathering dusk; being sent upstairs in winter by some adult to fetch something from an unlighted room; and, of course in bed; in bed, at dead of night or in the small hours when everyone else in the house was asleep. Then they became reality – fearful and terrifying.

Why was such a practice allowed? In some homes even the grimmer of Grimm's fairy tales were banned. Presumably it was because no child reported it – or if they did, lightly, and were in no way affected. Others, myself among them, kept quiet. Probably, again like myself, because they were fascinated by the stories, hanging breathlessly so to speak, on every horror.

That Mother St Bernard should have known better seems obvious. Grimm's – and most other fairy stories – were about strange people such as one never saw – and they had happened long ago. Ghost stories were of today; they could – evidently did, happen to all kinds of people; they might happen to people one actually knew . . . to oneself!

Why my parents never made any attempt to trace the cause of my so-called 'bad dreams' – something I continued to have at intervals throughout my years at the school – remains a mystery. To myself, at the time, there was also a mystery; the mystery of why, when a boarder, the night-mares ceased; a mystery only solved in later years when one realised one had been sleeping not in a room alone – or even with a dog, but in the company of an adult and a dozen or so companions.

* * * * *

Among other attractions of the later bed-time were the evening walks – especially in spring. The Convent was quite near the river – not far from its estuary. One of our walks took us nearer but over high ground so that although the river actually flowed beside us all the way we saw nothing of it.

We would set off two and two, in a 'crocodile', a couple of nuns chattering to each other in voluble French bringing up the rear. In less than ten minutes we were in what we called 'real country'. Here 1860 vanished for what greeted us was timeless; the heady – almost intoxicating – smell of Hawthorn blossom. In every hedge-row small trees and bushes were smothered in myriads of little white flowers, speckled with reddish pink and somehow reminding one of a well-made junket.

The nuns seemed to enjoy the almost cloying sweetness of the blossom as much as we did but kept exhorting us on no account to pick any, much less bring it into the house, a 'taboo' only too familiar to me from my mother. (What, one wonders, was the origin of this widespread, and so firmly held-to, superstition?)

In less than another ten minutes we came to some rough grassland overlooking the estuary. At high tide this was a broad, billowing sheet of water, at low tide reduced to a narrow channel filled with a slowly flowing stream, revealing the dry sandy beach of the village opposite, and a vast expanse of wet sand patterned with innumerable little sea-weed covered islands.

Permission to break up the 'crocodile' and run about and play was now given while the two nuns sat primly on a fallen log admiring the view. By the time the order to return was given the sun was beginning to sink low in the sky; there was the wonder of pinkish, gold-edged clouds and the twittering of small birds preparing to roost in hedges . . .

In twenty minutes we were back, surfeited with fresh air and Hawthorn blossom and hungry for the sparse evening meal. Five minutes later a lay-sister was vigorously ringing the supper bell. We were back again in 1860.

*　　*　　*　　*　　*

Very occasionally one or two of the day-boys – there were no boy boarders – would join us on one of these walks but I think they were not actively encouraged to do so. Boys were admitted to the school up to the age of eleven. On the whole they were well-behaved but, as in nearly every school there was one regular disturber of the peace. Philip was one of the younger members of a large local Roman Catholic family. Two of his older sisters led exemplary and blameless lives in the top form, under the redoubtable Mère St Madeleine. But Philip was a natural trouble-maker – especially as he grew older.

My earliest memory of him is a class-room incident during my first few weeks. A lay-teacher usually taught most subjects in this, the lowest class of all, but on the occasion in question she was away ill and a French nun, understanding but speaking very little English was in charge. There were three other boys in the class, two of them brothers who I remember well – if for rather dissimilar reasons. Firstly because their legs emerged from their dark-blue serge shorts clad in girls' stockings – brown ribbed ones; and secondly – something on which we were all agreed – they, or rather their parents, gave far the best parties of anyone we knew. The fourth boy was younger and so quiet one hardly knew he was there. His name was Ralph – sometimes pronounced Raif – according to the nationality of the speaker.

The incident in question took place on a raw, foggy, November morning. 'The Milk Rite' was over but there was an hour or so before what was known as 'Dismissal'. A reading lesson was in progress. Both the brown-stocking boys read well, likewise Eugénie and several others, Philip indifferently, myself very badly. The 'extract' chosen from the appointed 'Reading Book' was entitled, 'The Swedish Antarctic Expedition'. A harmless title one would have thought and with the prospect of some adventures to follow. I remember thinking they were very long words, and I was hazy as to the pronunciation of 'Antarctic' – or its exact meaning and that 'Exhibition' looked odd and that I would not have written it that way myself.

Philip was selected to begin. He stood up – one always stood to read one's 'piece', frowning furiously. Perhaps it was the weather; the milk extra sour, or, more likely a 'try on' to see how much the nun would put up with.

'The-Swedish-Antarctic-Expedition' he announced slowly. Then suddenly, and very quickly, he repeated the words. Finally, grinning broadly, round the class, one hand raised as if to conduct an orchestra, he half shouted, half chanted them.

There was no mistaking his meaning and suddenly the whole class — some fifteen or so – had joined in. 'The-Swedish-Antarctic-Expedition! *The-Swedish-Antarctic Expedition*!' . . . The din was terrific, the four boys making by far the most noise. In vain the nun did her best to restore order but seemed powerless. The noise became louder still – almost deafening. Clasping her hands together she stood helpless – gazing heaven-wards.

It has been said that 'instant prayer pierces Heaven' . . . At that moment Mère St Madeleine happened to be passing along the corridor outside. The door was flung open and she stormed into the room. The girls stopped chanting at once, the boys less quickly.

Though in many ways in advance of her time, Mère St Madeleine still believed in some old-fashioned nursery punishments. She wasted no time. There were four corners to the room and first in voluble French and then in English to make sure there should be no mistake, she directed one boy to each corner and finally, when all were installed issuing a stern warning against daring to move from them until she gave permission. She then swept out like a whirl-wind only to re-open the door a second later, hold up a warning finger and repeat her command.

Awed but thrilled the rest of us continued with our reading, though when, why or how 'The Swedish Antarctic Expedition' took place and what, if anything, befell those concerned with it, has long since vanished from my memory.

For a short time there was silence from the four corners. The reading droned on, the nun too intent on the readers to bother much over the culprits in the corners. But soon some of the class detected faint rolling and clinking sounds. Presently subdued giggles came from each of the four corners and every now and then one of the figures would bend down as if to retrieve something from the floor. Looking down, some of us could see little coloured balls were being rolled from one corner to another and very soon it was clear a game of marbles was in progress. Only when two of the players suddenly exploded with laughter did the nun look critically towards the four navy-blue jersey-clad backs, some now bent nearly double, partly with mirth and partly from grovelling for their own particular marbles. But before she had time to register any protest the 'Dismissal' bell began to ring. A second later and Mère St Madeleine was standing in the doorway while in each corner a red-faced boy struggled to stand upright . . .

As, according to custom, we all lined up to file out of the room, we listened almost breathless with suspense. The boys had been released and as we filed out Mère St Madeleine was telling them exactly what she thought of them; the certainty of white 'Primes' for all . . . But – no mention of marbles! Had she not seen those grovelling backs, those red faces? Or, for once, had something escaped her eagle eye? Very unlikely. Nevertheless marbles were definitely not mentioned – and certainly not seen – all now being safely in the pockets of their respective owners.

* * * * *

The climax in regard to boy-pupils came with Desmond. Desmond was twelve – over the age limit, and had only been admitted after much pleading on the part of his parents who, newly arrived in the district had discovered neither of the local boys' schools would accept their son until the following term. Eventually someone mentioned that The Convent 'took' boys.

Probably the fact that Desmond's mother, unlike his father, was a Roman Catholic helped to influence the Reverend Mother's decision. Desmond was accepted for the remainder of the present term; fortunately, as things turned out, about two-thirds over. All this took place after most of us had long since exchanged our emerald-green Cordelières for the dark-red ones that proclaimed our promotion to the class above, presided over by Mother St Bernard.

Desmond duly arrived. He was a very big boy for his age;

tall, broad – not to say fat, with fair wavy hair and the kind of smile often described in Victorian novels as 'bewitching'. He was – or appeared to be – appallingly backward, his reading efforts even worse than mine. He made not the slightest attempt to learn anything; denied any knowledge of French at all and was obviously determined not to acquire any. During his first few days he shared a desk with the younger of the brown-stocking boys whom he became absorbed in teasing in half-a-dozen different ways. In vain Mother St Bernard remonstrated. Desmond simply turned his 'bewitching' smile on her. At first she succumbed but it soon became evident his teasing was preventing his companion from learning anything either. Desmond was removed to a desk of his own.

Philip who, together with the other three boys was leaving at the end of the term, and who throughout his time at the school had considered himself the leader in all attempts to undermine discipline, quickly recognised a kindred spirit. They became great friends and one morning in close conversation during the Milk Rite, Desmond produced a small silver-like dagger. The other boys hovered near and presently they too were being drawn into whatever conspiracy was being hatched. No girls were included – and had no wish to be. Returning to the classroom for a History lesson we waited anxiously, expectantly. *Something* was about to happen – and very soon something did!

The lesson began; we were 'doing' the French Revolution – perhaps a rather suitable setting for what followed. For, drawing his dagger from its sheath and flourishing it menacingly in every direction, Desmond suddenly shot from his desk and swooping down on Philip stabbed him viciously in the chest with it!

One of the girls screamed and one or two burst into tears as the victim, with much clatter and groaning, fell to the floor.

Calmly leaning down and removing the dagger from his victim Desmond then pointed it at Mother St Bernard who, white as the proverbial sheet, had risen from her chair and now bravely pursued him to his desk. Here, before she could reach him he suddenly plunged the dagger into his own chest and slumping sideways rolled over to the floor.

The horror-stricken Mother St Bernard, torn between resuscitating Philip or Desmond chose the latter as being the nearer, only as she pulled the dagger from his chest to be greeted by hilarious laughter and the discovery that the weapon was a toy – if rather a sophisticated one! (Actually a kind then used by actors – and sometimes conjurers; the 'silver' blade being made of small – almost invisible – aluminium segments that folded back on each other when pressed against any hard surface, thereby giving the impression of having penetrated it.)

Leaving the weapon on her desk Mother St Bernard went quickly through the door in the wooden partition which separated the two lower class-rooms and after arranging with the lay-teacher in charge to 'keep an eye' on us, disappeared. In about five minutes she returned and announced to Desmond that the Reverend Mother wished to see him in her Parlour – at once. And, greatly to the surprise of us all, Desmond, the hilt of his dagger – which he had retrieved from Mother St Bernard's desk while she was away, sticking out of his pocket, got meekly to his feet and went!

The history lesson was resumed. Desmond did not return. The Dismissal bell rang and there was still no sign of him; neither did he appear at afternoon school. But not long before it ended, the Reverend Mother – who rarely visited a class-room, came in. Holding up a hand for silence she announced, very slowly and in her halting English, 'Desmond will not be returning to you. He has been *EX*-pelled!', and waiting a moment for it to sink in, left us.

*   *   *   *   *

A week or so later there was a 'Parent's Day' and before the end the Reverend Mother 'craved permission' as she put it, to make a short announcement. This was to the effect that since the four remaining boys were all leaving at the end of the present term, after much prayer and consultation it had been reluctantly decided that in future the school would no longer be accepting boys.

*   *   *   *   *

'But were you *happy* there?' I have sometimes been asked and my emphatic 'Yes' has often been received with surprise – even incredulity.

It was true and if I ask myself 'Why?' I think the short answer is in the one word 'stability'. There was always an indefinable sense of changelessness – of security, of certainty – matters of deep import to very young minds. The certainty, for instance, that Mère St Sacre-Coeur would peep through the grille and open the door at precisely 9.30 a.m.; that Mother St Bernard would be sitting smiling at her desk awaiting her morning quota of kisses; that good behaviour would be rewarded, bad punished, and that the fiery Mère St Madeleine would register her usual indignant displeasures. Then the security – the all-embracing sense of welcome, of kindliness; the sure sympathy . . . Above everything the all-pervading atmosphere of assured love; love given – love received . . .

Clutching my black pinafore and the decorated 'farewell' card referred to in First School (p. 150), I left – in tears.

The End

Epilogue

EVEN BEFORE I actually left The Convent, and as I have written, the German Kaiser's boastings and constant additions to his Fleet were becoming a frequent subject of conversation. Now rumour of war increased daily, eventually becoming reality. In the general slaughter of the next four years, contemporaries of my father; older friends of my sisters; an uncle, three cousins – one still in his teens – were drowned or killed, missing or maimed. A whole way of life was swept away, never to return; the remaining years of childhood irrevocably tarnished; the age of disillusion had arrived, the era of dissolution had begun.

* * * * *

When I began these chapters I quoted Wilfred Scawen Blunt who wrote at the turn of the century, and in all good faith, *'He who has once been happy, Is for aye out of destruction's reach! . . .'* But in the blood-stained and treacherous Today who can write with any confidence 'for aye', and the words of a later poet, unconsciously prophetic perhaps, may speak more truly.

'From quiet home and first beginning,
Out to the undiscovered ends,' wrote Hillaire Belloc,
*   'There's nothing worth the wear of winning*
But laughter – and the love of friends . . .'

KWASCHIK

WEST SUSSEX COUNTY LIBRARY

WITHDRAWN